The Mystery Fancier

Nov-Dec 1982   Vol.6·No.6

The Mystery Fancier

Volume 6, Number 6
November/December 1982

TABLE OF CONTENTS

MYSTERIOUSLY SPEAKING 1
Mae West: Mistress of Mystery?, by Billy Barton 2
To Be and Not to Be, by E.F. Bleiler. 3
Anne Morice: The Deadly Serious Business of Not Being
 Serious, by Neysa Chouteau and Martha Alderson. 5
Maps of Xiccarph, By Bob Sampson. 9
IT'S ABOUT CRIME, by Marvin Lachman 19
REEL MURDERS: Movie Reviews by Walter Albert. 23
MYSTERY*FILE: Short Reviews by Steve Lewis. 26
VERDICTS: More Reviews. 33
THE DOCUMENTS IN THE CASE: Letters. 40

The Mystery Fancier
(USPS:428-590)
is edited and published bi-monthly by
Guy M. Townsend
1711 Clifty Drive
Madison, IN 47250

SUBSCRIPTION RATES: Domestic second-class mail, $12.00 per year (six issues); first-class mail, U.S. and Canada, $15.00; overseas surface mail, $12.00; overseas airmail, $18.00. Overseas subscribers please pay in international money order, check drawn on U.S. bank, or currency; no checks drawn on foreign banks, please.

Single copy price: $2.50

Second class postage paid at Madison, Indiana

Copyright 1982 by Guy M. Townsend
All rights reserved for contributors
ISSN:0146-3160

I've a great deal to cover this time out and damned little space to do it in. The bad news first: this issue of TMF contains the final installment of Mystery*File. After six years and many hundreds of reviews, Steve Lewis has decided to take a rest. I can't blame him--I'd have burned out a hell of a lot sooner on half his load--but I'm sure going to miss him. I have a dozen or so of his reviews left over, and I'll work them into the Verdicts section of the next few issues so that we won't have to go cold turkey. I am hopeful that Steve will find other ways--such as articles and letters, as well as the odd review or two--to remain active in TMF, which in large part owes its existence to him. A glance at the nearly ten pages of entries under his name in last issue's index will give some idea of how important Steve has been to TMF.

Now some good news. You will have noted, probably with some relief, the absence of the pipe-smoking mystery fancier from this issue's cover. Brad Foster, who prepared this cover as well as the new department heads which you will find inside, has signed on as permanent cover artist for TMF. He has promised a new cover for every issue, and I am ecstatic. Any suggestions for future covers will be gladly passed on to him.

Back in 6:3 I recommended a new French publication to you people, but I did not at that time have complete information regarding subscription costs. I do now. Four issues of *Hard Boiled Dicks* can be had (via air mail) by sending $12 in cash to Roger Martin, 1, route d'Halanzy, Piedmont, 54350 Mont-Saint-Martin, FRANCE. Or, if you wish to pay by check, make it payable to Roger Martin, Account no. 31860040, Caisse Mutvelle de depots et de frêts, Place Leclerc Longwy 54400, FRANCE. The most recent issue, number four, has just arrived and is devoted to Joseph Hansen and Joe L. Hensley. HBD IS an outstanding publication, and even a smattering of high-school French will enable you to derive pleasure and information from it.

Ely Liebow is one of the most delightful people I have ever met. (His only flaw, to my knowledge, is a steadfast refusal to subscribe to this magazine.) He is also a dedicated and knowledgeable Sherlockian, and he has turned his considerable wit and intelligence to the task of producing a biography of *Dr. Joe Bell: Model for Sherlock Holmes*. The book runs to 256 pages and includes twenty-one photos and an index. Published by Bowling Green University's Popular Press (Bowling

(Continued on page 18)

Mae West: Mistress of Mystery? Almost...
By Billy Barton

Everyone in my show business world knows that Mae West and I were close friends. My father acted as her press agent for the play *Sex* in 1927 (the year of my birth), and when she had trouble getting the New York dailies to run ads with the show's title she journeyed to my family's circus, playing at the time in New Jersey, and grabbed our billposters to paper Manhattan. Each time city officials tore down the paper my family's stalwarts slapped it back up again. *Sex* became a smash hit and my association with Mae started at that instant, although it wasn't to flower until the 1950's when I went to work for her in her night club revue.

Mae and I saw a lot of each other over the years. I spent weekends at her beach house in Santa Monica when I was filming *Jumbo* at MGM, and she came often to circuses in which I was starring. Mae was a great circus fan. She adored circus people, was crazy about lions and tigers and monkeys.

In Mae's cast, during the production of *Catherine Was Great* and, later, during the revival of *Diamond Lil*, was a clever artist, Ray Bourbon, a female impersonator who played Mae's maid in *Catherine* and a beat-up bowery hag in *Lil*. During the run of *Lil*, Mae West and Ray Bourbon collaborated on a murder mystery play which was never produced.

In the 1960's, while I was writing material for Ray's new night club act, he asked me to refashion the script into a novel. I thought the play was too dated; besides, I knew absolutely nothing about crafting murder mysteries and wasn't remotely interested in writing mysteries, so I declined.

Worse, I gave him back the script which he had given to me!

The opus was called *Daddy Was a Lady*. The plot concerned a wealthy and famous female impersonator living in Soughhampton enroute to England for an important theatrical engagement. In the opening scene, while his wife and family awaited him downstairs, he is confronted by a blackmailer whom he murders and puts in one of the trunks bound for England. The plot then culminates in a hilarious mixture of murder and madness and mistaken identity which only a mind like Mae's, abetted by Ray's weird sense of humor, could invent.

Now that I *am* a mystery writer, with one book out and another on the way, I am regretful that I did not retain that script. I would turn it into a novel, put the names of Mae West and Ray Bourbon on the cover, and publish it as a curiosity piece if nothing else. *(Continued on page 18)*

To Be and Not to Be
By E.F. Bleiler

Far-out theories apart, there is a fair degree of consensus among the moderns who have tried to work out the solution to Charles Dickens' unfinished mystery, *The Mystery of Edwin Drood*. Dickens, it will be remembered, died when the story was about half finished and left no significant notes or indications of what would happen. Future events have had to be reconstructed out of hints from within the story and from the memories of Dickens' friends and family. These memories are very scanty, since Dickens was secretive about the work.

The agreement among moderns, basically, is: (1) that Edwin Drood was murdered (Dickens admitted this to four people, including the two artists that worked with him); (2) that John Jasper, Drood's nearly coetaneous uncle, murdered him; (3) that Jasper's crime would be revealed through converging suspicions and investigations. Most students also believe that at the end of the book there was to have been (4) a confrontation between Jasper and someone disguised as the dead Drood (probably Helena Landless), and (5) that there was to have been a chase up the cathedral tower, in connection with which (somehow or other) Neville Landless was to be killed by Jasper. And (6) that Jasper would be taken by Tartar and others.

In *The Decoding of Edwin Drood* (Scribner's, 1980), Charles Forsyte (an unrevealed pseudonym) accepts the general agreement above with one major exception, which is his contribution to Drood speculation. Forsyte believes that Jasper murdered Drood, but also that Jasper was innocent of the murder.

Forsyte argues that Jasper was a true, extreme case of multiple personality, John Jasper proper and John Jasper the Murderer, between whom there is no communication. Thus, when the Murderer kills Drood, Jasper does not know of it. Actually, Forsyte is by no means the first to advance this theory, which goes at least as far back as 1927 (to Eustace Conway's "Mystery of Edwin Drood" in *Anthony Munday and Other Essays*), but Forsyte's typological significance lies in developing the thesis in much greater detail and with further ramifications than previous solutions.

A reminiscence of John Forster, Dickens' friend and confidant, serves as the basis for Forsyte's theory. Forster claimed that Dickens had told him that at the end of the novel Jasper was to tell his story "as if, not he, the culprit, but some other man were the tempted." Forsyte builds on this and interprets much of what goes on in the novel, not as it seems on the surface, but as material with a hidden, double meaning. Thus, he takes Jasper's persecution of Neville Landless for the disappearance of Drood not as hypocrisy or safety-first (as it is usually taken), but as sincere belief on Jasper's part. Jasper, says Forsyte, really believes that Landless killed Drood, since Jasper does not know what the Murderer has done. Forsyte sees the theme of double personality as pervading the book, even to the minor characters. Most of Forsyte's argument here is very forced and unconvincing.

As to the primary point of Forsyte's book--that Jasper is a true double personality--I remain somewhat incredulous, though, as happens with most theories about *Drood*, one can find a little evidence for it, but not enough to carry any conviction. Some say that the reason for this elusiveness of the text lies in Dickens' art; others, that it is evidence that Dickens was cracking up mentally, as he undoubtedly was physically.

A problem that Forsyte and his predecessors have not faced squarely is the historical status of double personality around 1870. One can find evidence of secondary personalities associated with drugs of one sort or another in medicine and literature (like Franklin Blake in *The Moonstone* or Margrave in Bulwer-Lytton's *A Strange Story*, both of which Dickens had published and knew well), but this is not the same thing as multiple personality. Multiple personality in the sense that Forsyte postulates seems to have been isolated considerably later than the 1870's. Morton Prince comes to mind.

I find it impossible to swallow Forsyte's theory in all its ramifications. My own opinion is that one can accept Forster's statement by recognizing either a secondary drug personality for Jasper or a complete breakdown in which Jasper writes of his crime as if committed by another person.

The oddest evidence that Forsyte puts forth for the circumstances and fate of John Jasper lies in his analysis of two passages that Dickens inserted as fillers within the action. One passage describes the food storage facilities at Canon Crisparkle's establishment, the other a herb closet maintained by Crisparkle's mother. Forsyte sees these passages as parables of Jasper and his fate. He picks out isolated words within them and claims that Dickens was subliminally building up a statement that Jasper would be confined in a prison cell, where he would commit suicide upon learning what he has done.

This, of course, is simply absurd, for one can pull isolated words out of a long passage to make a case for almost anything, if one reads them subliminally according to a preconceived system of reference. Nor does Forsyte offer any explanation as to why these passages are written about Crisparkle (wholesomeness) and not Jasper. (They appear in Dickens' "number notes" as "The closet I remember there as a child.")

After the argument, which takes up about half of the book, Forsyte undertakes a fictional expansion of his ideas, thus joining the company of those who have tried to finish *Drood*. In this "sequel," Helena Landless, disguised as the dead Drood, confronts Jasper; Neville Landless is killed by being tossed from the tower; and Crisparkle and Tartar capture Jasper. So far, this is not unconventional. The novelty appears in Jasper's fate. The Murderer component in the prison cell talks openly of his crime to Crisparkle, but the Jasper-proper com-

(Continued on page 18)

Ann Morice
The Deadly Serious Business of Not Being Serious
By Neysa Chouteau and Martha Alderson

Felicity Shaw seems to be a relatively demure if somewhat puckish wife, mother, and grandmother. As Anne Morice, she is a killer.

Anne Morice's mystery novels appeal to readers who are fond of the classic British mystery style, of humor, or of both. Even when Morice's novels are set in Paris or Washington, they remain unquenchably British. Their humor springs primarily from sharp observations of human frailty described in colorful metaphors.

We interviewed Morice at her village home near Henley-on-Thames in Oxfordshire on a bright warm May afternoon, a setting as British as a travel poster. Morice's outward manner was more self-effacing than that of Tessa Crichton, the brash young actress who is the amateur sleuth featured in all of Morice's mystery novels. Morice was, however, every bit as cheerful, mischievous, and adept with a phrase as Tessa. She may even have been as devious. She set us laughing so often that we did not have time to ask all our questions.

While the interview was both fun and funny, it revealed that Morice is quite serious about her work. She writes every day. "It's silly, really. But I feel if I'd break the habit, I'd never get back to it. But if you once sort of break the discipline, you think 'Why the hell should I work? It's a lovely day. I'll go for a walk or stay in bed.' I write very early in the morning. I get up about 5:30 in the morning. It's the only time when you're absolutely free. Not just free from interruptions but free from self-imposed pressures, like what shall we have for lunch or ought I to be, you know, tidying up the kitchen or the sort of thing that takes over.

"And I find that even shopping lists take something out of your creative effort. At that time of morning your mind is clear."

Morice works two hours at most, sometimes only twenty minutes. Her goal, which she says she seldom achieves, is about five hundred words a day.

When she referred to herself as a slow writer, we pointed out that she had published more than a book a year for some years (seventeen books in twelve years, to be exact).

"Well, I think I'm a slow writer, and yet I can never give myself a day off. I'm not one of those who wait for inspiration because if I'd wait for it, I'd wait forever, and suddenly write three thousand words. I write every day, a certain amount, and it gets done. It works out. Every book is exactly the same length, around sixty thousand words, and it takes exactly the same number of days to write it and the same number of corrections and recorrections. It works out inevitably the same for each book. It simply happens that way. I don't set myself a target."

Few women can discuss work for long without touching upon the special problems of working women. We asked Morice if her three children were grown when she started writing.

"When my youngest child was about six months old, we went to a station abroad and had maximum service. That was when I started to write as a regular thing. But, of course, I am lucky, because I've been able to do it.

"I am a feminist, actually. I think it's such a shame there's so much talent, far more talent than I've got, which is not really developed, not even known about. It's a shame, isn't it, that more women can't? If I were a man, people wouldn't dare ring me up and say, 'I don't mean to interrupt you,' would they?

"You see, most of us are so diffident that we're not quite sure we've got enough to justify being selfish and rude and uncivilized about that. If I were certain I had a lot of talent, I'd tell them all to go and shoot themselves. But I keep trying to compensate for the fact that I'm living a dream half my life by being, you know, patient. 'How are you, darling? Do you want to go to the station? Is your girlfriend coming?' That sort of thing, because ... that's being a woman, isn't it? Deferent, always, isn't it?"

Morice wrote two "straight" novels, as she called them, before she turned to writing mysteries. The switch came when her husband, Alex Shaw, was stationed in Paris.

"I used to commute. That was easy. It's only about forty minutes. I used to spend a month there and a month home. When I got to Paris, everyone would say, 'Any new Penguins brought with you? Crime stories?' That's when I wrote the first one. I thought, 'Tremendous demand for these, not enough to go around, so I'll write one.'

"When I got back I read that they were giving a prize at Macmillan [London] for mysteries. I thought, 'If they are doing that--giving out money--they certainly want new writers, so this is the moment.' I sent it to them, and they published it. Easy as falling off a log."

Morice's easy first success and her sustained track record have not increased her confidence. In fact, just the opposite.

"I think that the more successful I get, the more I feel it's a bit of a con, in a way. 'Okay,' I say, 'Why shouldn't I work jolly hard? Why shouldn't I earn three hundred quid?' And as it grows and grows and is translated and in paperback and so on, I think, "When are they going to find me out?'"

Morice had great fun writing her first mystery, *Death in the Grand Manor*. "I wrote it for a lark, and there was never that much fun again." She finds that the fun of writing each succeeding book has varied tremendously, and in unpredictable ways. "I think it's a matter of getting interested in the characters straight away--straight away. Not building them up afterwards. But really seeing them, feeling them, believing in them immediately."

Morice uses continuing characters in her mysteries: Tessa

Chrichton Price, her husband, Robin Price of the C.I.D., her eccentric cousin, Toby Crichton, and others. We asked about the problems of using continuing characters.

"Obviously, the main one is you have to remember that a great number of people are reading this story who've never read any others. Therefore, you have to establish these characters. So the main problem is establishing them without being too repetitive for the one or two readers who know them well. You have to make that balance between establishing their backgrounds and characters without being boring to the constant readers and absolutely incomprehensible to the new reader; it would, of course, be very rude to new readers to assume they would know. So, that's the difficulty.

"I've tried to break away once or twice. But--the publishers are a shock to me--they say, 'Oh. no, you see, people like your characters, and they'd be disappointed. It's not fair. You can't put families in a book and then have an entirely different set of characters.' And I see what they mean."

Morice is grateful that readers like her characters, but she says "it's just that now and then I'd like to get away from this. It's just lethargy, really. Everything has to be written from the point of view of this young woman."

As to the rewards of using continuing characters, Morice says, "It's a short cut for me. I've got them established when I start. I know what their reactions are going to be. I don't have to build them up in order to build them up for the reader. You see, you have to first of all create them in your own mind in order to recreate them for the reader. You are already there."

Morice has biographies in mind for all her characters, even the minor ones, although the biographies are not written down. "I have them all in my head. I know where they live and what they look like and what they do. I have to check back to earlier books to find names and things like that. I can't remember if Mackintosh is called Mackintosh in the first book and that sort of thing. But as figures and people and faces, I have them."

Tessa, Morice's main character, is an actress because "the only subject I have any technical knowledge at all of is the theater. So, I introduce that, and it is useful because an actress can get around anywhere. Not only get around anywhere but be accepted in places where one of her own age and looks and circumstances and that sort of thing would not be allowed to get. But people--a lot of them--are stage struck and really impressed by anybody who's been on the television. So Tessa gets away with an awful lot of things that an ordinary young woman would not."

Morice poked gentle fun at the whole notion of a technical background and its importance to critics.

"Critics are rather strange. They always like to have an authentic, well-researched background. I think it has something to do with not reading books for pleasure. I don't think critics like books. Therefore, they feel books are absolutely a waste of time unless readers are learning something. The idea of reading for sheer entertainment is anathema and goes against the Puritan tradition. As long as they're learning something, even if it's how to draw up a beer, it's okay. Even with a background like the theater, they feel they're learning something which as members of the audience they wouldn't see. I think that the more theatrical background there is, the more time that's wasted on padding--the rehearsal took four hours, and so on--the more the critics feel this is something they're learning.

"Not all critics, but some."

Morice's own views as to what a mystery novel should be are quite different from those she ascribes to critics. "I think that crime stories, mystery stories, and all that should be read at a swallow. They're just like a crossword puzzle. If you can't fill in number 24, you say, 'Well, all right, I'll go to bed and I'll do that tomorrow.' You never do. I think that's the fun of it, really, the fun of reading mysteries, don't you? When they try to get sort of serious and meaningful, the game's over. It's not the same. Then it's not for reading in an airplane. I'm strictly for reading in an old chair."

The fact that Morice feels strongly that mysteries are for casual reading does not mean that she is casual about her work. We asked her why she now writes only mysteries.

"Because I like the discipline of it. It's rather like painting a picture and putting the frame on the canvas before you start. Within that framework you can do anything as long as you've got a nice picture. But you can't paint over the frame and onto the walls behind it. And I would tend to do that, I think. But as long as I've got this rigid thing to stick to, the plot, it's got to have a murderer and so many suspects and logical reason and all that sort of thing, I'm stuck with it and that's good for me, because otherwise it would go all askew."

So far as the work is concerned, Morice states that "It's dead serious, absolutely dead serious. And it could not be more. But, of course, the end result is like a good joke. You know, like a comedian, a standup comic. I mean, God knows the blood, sweat and tears that he puts into it. Three lines, maybe. The joke is supposed to be thrown away and send one into gales of laughter for only two seconds. It's serious work, isn't it? Otherwise, he doesn't send you into gales of laughter. I mean, he might just as well go home and take up some other job."

We then began to ask questions about specific points in certain books. The formal interview ended when, in response to one question, Morice replied, "Cut off your machine."

What we asked and what she answered, we will leave a mystery.

[All of Anne Morice's mysteries have been published in England by Macmillan; beginning with *Death and the Dutiful Daughter*, they have also been published in the United States by St. Martin's. They are: *Death in the Grand Manor* (1970), *Murder in Married Life* (1971), *Death of a Gay Dog* (1971), *Murder on French Leave* (1972), *Death and the Dutiful Daughter* (1973), *Death of a Heavenly Twin* (1974), *Killing with Kindness* (1974), *Nursery Tea and Poison* (1975), *Death of a Wedding Guest* (1976), *Murder in Mimicry* (1977), *Scared to Death* (1978), *Murder by Proxy* (1978), *Murder in Outline* (1979), *Death in the Round* (1980), *The Men in Her Death* (1981), *Hollow Vengeance* (1982), and *Sleep of Death* (to be published in 19820.]

Maps of Xiccarph
By Bob Sampson

Steve's Magazine Exchange occupied inconspicuous quarters two blocks off the downtown business district of Charleston, West Virginia.

On Saturdays, early in 1940--weather and parents permitting--you rode your bicycle into the deeps of town. You cut past the hulking gray library, followed right as the street jogged between smoke-stained office buildings, then straight ahead through the main intersection, small and cluttered, the YMCA at the left on an intersecting street that led off past department stores, dime stores, jewelers, tailors, and merchants, to the narrow highway paralleling the Kanawaha River.

But your business took you elsewhere. One arm gripping a brown paper sack containing assorted pulp magazines and comic books, you pedaled into that fringe of small, starved stores girdling the business district. For years, this area had slowly withered, and business was conducted with the air that it would probably all be over next week.

Shoe-shine parlors and barber shops clustered here. Down the street waited the credit clothing stores, their windows bright with interest-ridden shoddy. Beyond fumed a grubby lunch room where a nickle bought two hot dogs, Today Only. Then a drugstore, its windows caked with excited signs. Next door stood a moving picture theatre no larger than a cracker box. It featured two westerns, a newsreel, short subjects, prevues, and (on Saturday) a serial part--ten cents a ticket, and you could stay to watch everything twice.

At the end of the street, where squalor faded insensibly into failure, you found the Magazine Exchange.

It was a narrow-fronted shop, the two small display windows separated by a recessed doorway. To the window glass were plastered inexpertly lettered signs offering the current exchange rates--two or three of yours for one of his. On Saturday, the store frontage was piled with bicycles as enterprising traders tried their luck.

In the right display window, comics rose in ragged piles, either coverless or the next thing to it. Flanking them sprawled stacks of western, detective, and love pulps, and a selection of Big Little Books that had been read violently.

In the left window heaped the big slick-paper magazines--*Collier's*, *Life*, *Liberty*, *Better Homes and Gardend*, *Field and Stream*, *Saturday Evening Post*--and countless women's magazines, their covers adorned by photographs of tailored ladies with highly polished faces.

You entered a long room. The air smelled richly of old paper, seasoned by whiffs of toilet. In the aisles, a babble of boys, pre-teens and older, scuffled and yawped, their feet thuding the worn linoleum.

"Cummere. Hey, cummere, look at this. Cummere."

"Ah, I saw that one."

"Hey, cummere."

Shelves solidly filled the right wall. They were built of unpainted pine boards, there being no frills at Steve's. They towered overhead, eight feet high, running twenty feet back to join tall shelves at the rear. There the shelving was pierced by an entrance to secret areas denied young customers. Over the entrance hung a curtain of limp brown stuff which occasionally fell awry, disclosing mouth-watering stacks of boxes. These brimmed with magazines. Bits of cover and miscellaneous pages littered the floor.

To your left was a plain wooden counter. Across it the comic books strewed. Behind the counter were shelves to the ceiling filled with innumerable issues of *Popular Science* and such controlled titles as *Spicies, Saucy, Breezy Stories*--issues whose subject matter was too vivid for pre-teen trade.

In this section Steve himself stumped back and forth. He was a short man, square and brown, lacking hair, and with a massive limp that caused his shoulders to pitch as he moved from deal to deal. His eyes were blue ice, his voice loud.

Three long tables packed the center floor area. These had been economically cobbled together from scrap lumber. You brushed along the table edges, ignoring the immediate danger of jabbing your chest full of splinters.

Across the first two tables spilled a tide of slick magazines--movie and confession magazines, their stories promising much but revealing only maple-nut centers; outdoors magazines across whose covers deer/bass/quail flaunted themselves before hunters. The table end was filled with *Life* magazine, gray-toned pictorial covers ornamented by the fat red bottom strip. And here lay *Fortune, Liberty,* modeling magazines (full of instructions about construction of immense, rubber-powered aircraft), and a litter of back-issue radio publications showing the true faces of Stella Dallas, Lum and Abner, Bob Burns.

But who lingered over these conventional pleasures?

It was the third table that drew you--that sprawling feast. Pulp magazines possessed it completely. Here newly acquired magazines were temporarily stacked until their slow assimilation by the shelves--at some distant time when business slacked off. And here, also, were the bargains--crippled magazines bereft of cover and spine, lacking pages, rat-gnawed or insect-ridden or read by enthusiasts who underlined with red crayon. These were "Two for 5¢."

All bore stamped upon their faces a legend in black ink:

STEVE'S MAGAZINE EXCHANGE
2 for 1
Current Magazines 5 Cents

Braving splinters, you slid along this table, all eyes and excitement. But first things necessarily came first.

You advanced to the counter and emptied your grocery sack,

laying out the trade material to Steve's unsympathetic inspection.
"What you do with these things, kid? Chew 'em?"
"Well ...."
"What juh want?"
"Wanna look around first."
You left your offerings in custody (how small and tattered your issues seemed) and turned away after only a glance at strews of Plastic Man Bulletman Superman Batman *Pep Whiz Detective Action.* You moved directly across the room to the right wall.

Here was the purpose of the trip. Here the recognized heart of your life, your joy and your despair.

Here the limitless pulp magazines stacked tall. The heart reeled with desire.

So many. So many. Choice numbed you.

No particular order was observed. Enough that detective magazines were shelved together: yellow-spined *Dime Detective,* white-spined *Detective Fiction Weekly, Black Mask* with scarlet or blue spines, *Clues, Private Detective, Ace G-Man.*

Here an entire section of *Argosy,* white spined with red or black letters. Ten or twenty years of *Argosy.* The thicker *Argosy All-Story Weekly*s filled the upper shelves, mingled with *Blue Book, Short Stories,* and such ancient strays as *Cavalier.* At the very top of the shelves, unreachable and, apparently, unsellable, you could see *The Popular Magazine,* dusty and neglected, and *Top Notch* and *People's*--the family magazines whose line extended back to the morning of the pulps, when all the family read and a magazine contained a story for each family member.

Here the western stories, the covers all somehow alike, showing a clench-jawed wrangler, with and without blood streaks, blasting his big Colt six. Next, a battered shelf of *Dare-Devil Aces, Wings, Air Trails, Sky Fighters,* seasoned by a handful of tattered *Battle Stories.* War had become a popular subject at the end of the 1920's; the air-war magazines survived down through the 1940's, the Spads transformed into Spitfires.

Then *Amazing Stories,* new issues an inch thick, their back covers paintings of off-world marvels. These mixed with scrambled issues of *Startling Stories, Thrilling Wonder Stories, Planet Stories.* On their covers, partially clothed spacemaidens posed as blasters roared to save them from tusked alien horrors. In the back, those promising boxes might contain *Wonder* or *Science Wonder Stories* or perhaps the big, white-spined *Amazing Stories Quarterly.* Only rarely did you see those; the science-fiction magazine was not yet fifteen years old, but, at Steve's, anyway, you didn't often find the large format. A determined reader could finger more *Astounding Science Fiction* and *Astounding Stories* than he could carry out.

You worked carefully down the shelves, sampling covers, reading titles. You did not realize it at the time, but here, towering over you, spreading out on each side, was a sampling of the reading tastes in popular fiction for the past twenty-five years.

Up by the ceiling, those few issues of *Detective Story Magazine* represented the beginning of the magazine devoted to detective and crime fiction. It began in the mid-'Teens and ran in unbroken, weekly sequence into the 1940's, to expire in years not yet lived. Then came *Black Mask*, and then *Flynn's-Flynn's Weekly-Flynn's Weekly Detective Fiction-Detective Fiction Weekly*, getting more violent with each issue and title change. And, developing in parallel, magazines of weirdly bloody adventures: *Detective Dragnet* and *Ten Detective Aces*, then *Dime Detective*. And, still later, G-men magazines, the titles adapting to the newspaper headlines.

Popular Detective, Thrilling Detective, Clues Detective. But as you read these titles your eyes kept straying to the shelves at the back of the shop. For on those shelves glowing patches of color, entirely distinctive, marked the rows of single-character pulp magazines.

So, at last, your heart rose large in you. You turned away, indifferent to the shelved columns of *Adventure*, the incredible libraries of *Romantic Range* and *Wild West Weekly* and *Western Story* (these rooted in the dime novels, although you didn't know that and didn't care). You hurried toward the end of the room, drawn by *The Spider*'s scarlet blaze, the orange spines of *Doc Savage*, the blue or red letters of *The Shadow*.

Now the serious searching began.

Doc Savage slashes a hand grenade up through a glass window.

The Spider, masked and desperate, jets blow-torch flame into the eye of a killer robot.

Three thugs, clutching gigantic .45's, peer toward a solitary walker; in the sky above them hovers The Avenger's immense face.

The Shadow whirls pistol first into a group of hooded fiends.

G-8 scrambles for a dropped Luger--as a gigantic, metal-headed creature heaves up a slugging rifle--as a sinister dwarf triggers a sinister machine--as a net is hurled to ensnare a rescuing Spad.

The Ghost, young, determined, tuxedoed, towers symbolically above a city skyline, his hands gripping wriggling crooks.

So very many titles.
How could you ever choose?
Full of anxiety, you raced along the shelves. At any moment, some intruding hand might snatch up a coveted treasure.

You pulled out the magazines in blocks, running swiftly through the stack, checking the covers. Before you had looked over all the *Doc Savages*, *The Spider* drew you. Before you completed *The Spider*, you moved to *G-8 and His Battle Aces*. Then to *The Shadow*.

The sheer volume dulled your appetite. To many issues clamoured for attention and numbed your eagerness. It would have been difficult to select from fifty *Doc Savage*s. But on these shelves also waited eighty *Shadow*s, thirty *Spider*s, ten or more *Avenger*s.

Many were duplications. Many more bore unacceptable damage. Many similar issues already lay boxed under your bed.

But the residue, the unfamiliar others ....

Among *The Shadows* you find two--no, three--copies of "Death's Premium," all badly treated. "City of Shadows," "Voice of Death." Then a flash of unfamiliar orange: "The Voice," on the cover The Shadow clinging to a wall, firing down. Some crazy has created bullet strikes about The Shadow by thrusting a pencil point repeatedly into the cover.

And here a lightly worn issue, the cover showing a partially clad woman, masked, with gun. But how much rather would you have had a picture of The Shadow.

On this shelf the scarlet-backed *Spider*s wait, fiercely illustrated.

"The Corpse Broker," "Satan's Murder Machines," "Blight of the Blazing Eye."

Many duplicates here. Cover edges are tattered and pages ride free of their staples, as if the intense story had burst free of restraint. Scribbled across the title page of "Rule of the Monster Men" are the words, "This is the best story I ever read."

And leagues of *Doc Savage*--shelf after shelf of the familiar orange spine with white ends, the title, *Doc Savage,* in vivid yellow.

"Mad Mesa," "The Green Death," Hex." And again "Hex." "Poison Island," "The Other World"--four issues of "The Other World."

Large numbers of *Doc Savage* circulated through Steve's. The magazine was widely read and, if condition were an indicator, read intensely. Various dates mingled on the shelves, the compact, trimmed, 1940's issues shuffled in with larger issues from 1938-1939, their edges rough. You noticed the difference without wondering about it.

Only rarely did any date earlier than 1938 show up. To find those you needed to fish less turbulent water than Steve's. Still, you checked by habit, remembering that tight, glossy, unmarred issue of "He Could Stop the World" you had found one notable Saturday. But such events were rare.

Your hands now gripped a precious small stack of magazines. Few enough, yet more than your pocket change and trade material could secure. Holding these issues close under your arm, you scanned those many other titles: *Phantom Detective, G-8, The Lone Eagle*. A copy of *Captain Future*. A few stray issues of *Secret Agent X Detective Mysteries*. A few *Operator 5*'s. Your fingers slipped across their bright promise, their fascination pulling at you physically, so immediate and so unobtainable.

From this glory you turned, choked by poverty; spread out your stack to make the final selections; culled ruthlessly; then turned toward the counter and Steve's cold arithmetic.

At length you left the store. You were stripped of pocket change and trade material, but in your hand you carried six unread magazines.

Six magazines!

As you wheeled back across Charleston, joy foamed in you.

So much material swarmed Steve's shelves that it appeared obvious the single-character magazine had always existed. The fact was self evident. In the golden afternoon of the pulp era, you bought and read, quite innocent of history. You selected all the magazines you could afford, whenever you could find them. They always had been there. They always would be there.

At this time only a few, highly favored people had checklists. No listing in any way complete was available to you. The early titles of your favorite magazine were unobtainable, unknown, unguessed, barring scattered titles mentioned in the "Letters" column.

Nor had you any idea that these varied titles, brightly dressed in vividly high-action covers, each concealed a private history: that men wrote them and other men edited and illustrated them; that they were created as items in a magazine chain; that they glimmered like dreams, dependent on the acceptance of readers in the United States and Canada; that they borrowed from one another and played endless variations on a few ideas.

You read of caped avengers, geniuses with guns, adventurers bristling with science-fictional devices, clever young disguise artists, masked crime solvers, secret service heroes, fairly naked jungle men ....

That these people and these magazines descended from the dime novels never occurred to you. You had never seen a dime novel. And if Steve had been offered a boxfull, he wouldn't have wasted shelf space on them. Fragile pamphlets dated 1890 and 1905 formed no part of his business, whether or not they were the root stock of the single-character magazines.

Each character whose adventures clutched your attention represented a certain line of fictional adventure. You might notice that The Avenger contained strong whiffs of Doc Savage, but you did not know that The Avenger's plastic face continued a literary tradition of long duration, including in its lineage the pliable features of Hamilton Cleek (1914) and, even earlier, that remarkable confidence man, Colonel Clay (1897).

Nor did you realize that the caped, sinister figures, The Shadow and The Spider, were modern representatives of a visual image more than 100 years old--that of the mystery figure, laughing weirdly, gliding in darkness.

These lines of evolution were quite invisible to the reader. The devices, the images, the character traits themselves, had been structured slowly over decades of popular fiction in a way that would be hard to believe were it not laid down in the published record.

Prior to the single-character magazine boom, you could find:
  --deadly heroes
  --wealthy heroes with secret identities
  --costumed heroes
  --deadly, secret, costumed fiends of malignant mind, who
     killed, plotted, destroyed, aided by legions of
     minions
  --clever investigators who prowled disguised
  --gangsters and their mobs blasting away
  --giddy movement of characters in up-to-date automobiles,
     airplanes, boats
  --scientific equipment and advanced technology
  --crimes committed by apparently supernatural causes.

In short, the 1920's cooked the dinner that was served all through the 1930's. But, then, every decade prepares for the next, and each shapes the stones that will, in ten years, be pieced into strange monuments.

In all the furious boiling and bubbling of 1920's fiction, some changes proceeded more quietly--almost, you might say, inadventently. These changes were occurring to the medium of pulp-magazine fiction, itself. But few enough people, at the time, observed the pale brightening of the future, heralding the coming of the hard-boiled action story and the arrival of the lethal hero.

The notorious pulp magazine narrative style--short sentences and unrelenting action--evolved in complicated ways. One day a person of energy and penetrating wisdom will work out how the pulps developed their characteristic sound. The final work will be in nine volumes and each of you will have a set on your shelves, very likely. Until that time, it may satisfy your questing mind to suggest that the 1930's pulp style contained memories of dime novels and English 1890's adventure romances, of *Argosy* and Hearst newspaper columns and Sherwood Anderson and Sinclair Lewis, of the late 1920's *Black Mask* and Ernest Hemingway. Plus techniques borrowed from the silent movies and the stage, with a very few radio elements thrown in. An enticing tangle.

Such a sketchy summary can only arouse the ire of those who know how much has been left out and who will hotly attest to the dominating importance of writers they greatly admire. They will be correct. To reach a reasonable understanding of how the 1930's single-character magazines got that way, you must back-track several different lines of literary development which interact with headcracking complications.

For our purposes, however, the strange joys of developmental analysis need not be encountered. Let's limit ourselves to the sub-sub-species of the mystery adventure story and two of its several main branches: the mystery-problem novel and the hardboiled novel.

The mystery-problem novel was a characteristic 1920's production. A crime problem was given and the hero undertook to solve it. The pace was leisurely, the influence English; the action ambled through meadows of words. The hero was a fine representative of his class, if eccentric; the police slow but good-hearted; and the society in which all this took place was sound at the core. The crime, you see, was no more than a splinter. Pluck it from society's hide and once again stability and decorum reigned.

In contrast, the hardboiled mystery novel was hot-paced, cold-eyed, and its main problem often seemed less who-done-it than how the hero was to survive to the end of the case. The hardboiled hero, a sardonic and inelegant fellow, scratched a living from a society demoralized, corrupt, and ferocious. The stories played up violence by violent men; that was presented as an accurate portrayal of the real world, only lightly dramatized for the dime-magazine market. If the lead figure could accomplish anything at all, it was because he could function in this world while alienated from its purpose, and because he adhered silently to such archaic standards as decency, integrity, and self sacrifice--all held in contempt by those around him. In the hands of Hammett, Nebel, and Chandler, these stories radiated authority. They affirmed an individual's personal worth, under certain circumstances, in a world denying it. The more conventional mysteries entertained; the hardboiled mysteries purified.

Almost from the beginning, the hardboiled mystery split into two main lines. That line exemplified by Hammett eventually received a morsel of literary recognition. The other line, pioneered by Carroll John Daly, received more scorn than anything else, although it proved more popular. It was easier to read, less unsettling, and a lot easier to write. This was the story of action--action, violence, and not a great deal of anything else.

Action was the key word. Blind, continuous action. Action at the expense of character development. Action that blandly ignored such real-world constraints as bleeding after being shot, being hospitalized after being hit on the head, and being arrested for public gunfights.

The Daly cast of characters performed in a world that did not quite exist. They were action figures in action stories. In this fiction, physical movement and violence became ends in themselves, the true purpose of the adventure. Realistic touches were allowed only if they did not interfere with the action, as it dashed from one bloody climax to the next.

Consider the glittering example of *Dime Detective* fiction ....

On the 20th of each month, early in 1932, the new issue of *Dime Detective* shown from the magazine racks. The light yellow title, outlined in scarlet, glowed above cover scenes of Terror, horror, death, all painted in luminous greens, blues, and light red, bright red, scarlet.

Within the magazine, the prose glowed as luminously.

There, death walked queerly. Weird entities slaughtered from a mist of supernatural fear. Bloody talons scratched night windows. In deadly silent houses, corpses sprawled and shining awfuls glided toward new prey.

By the end of the story, the gaping reader would learn that all this was window dressing. Monsters were the bunk. The supernaturalism was only frosting spread thick over conventional greed. For although *Dime Detective* toyed with atmospheric terror, its motives were solidly set in the cash box.

The prose generated its own effect--the sense that reality had melted at the edges, that no longer did you quite dare to predict what lay in the closet or waited in the corridor, listening to your breathing.

Even when the simulated supernatural did not tickle the story edges, the *Dime Detective* world was neither predictable nor safe. In this world, people died in numbers and for no good reason. Guns blared. Killers hacked their victims. And detectives, unsentimental as iron skillets, pursued the killers.

Vee Brown, for example, that remarkable, demi-official manhunter. Brown was another face from Carroll John Daly's detective stable and continued the tradition of Race Williams and Satan Hall. Which is to say, Brown's gun never cooled as, with irrepressible zeal, he shot the scoundrels down.

Frederick Nebel's Cardigan, of the Cosmos Agency, was not quite as murderous as Brown. But he was at least twelve times as tough. Cardigan moved through laconic stories sliced from the heartwood of the hardboiled detective style. His adventures sparkled with an angry simplicity. Killing did not overly fuss Cardigan; he would shoot as necessary.

These characters were in the tradition of the armed hero,

long an element of American fiction.

In the distant past, behind those pallid mists separating dime novels from the mystery pulps, Nick Carter had shot his man--in self defense. As early as 1907, Edgar Wallace's Just Men had organized as an efficient murder circle, the better to deal with recalcitrants refusing the discipline of English law. And Bulldog Drummond, a decade later, slugged and shot the ungodly with lordly righteousness.

But these men were exceptions. During the 'Teens and 'Twenties, most detective and mystery fiction heroes were denied the solace of lethal action. It was a curious limitation not affecting heroes of western or adventure fiction. Through these stories, the hero habitually blasted his way from chapter to chapter, leaving behind a trail of exploded cartridges and unburied losers.

In mystery fiction, however, the taboo held solidly. Dozens of lead characters promenaded the columns of *Street & Smith Detective Story Magazine* and *Detective Tales*, and not one would kill deliberately. If, occasionally, an accident happened and the gun went off, then the hero was condemned to hot agonies of conscience.

No, indeed. A lead mystery character would not shoot another human being. Not even a leering murderer. Not even a leering murderer soaked in blood, who threatened to kill the sweet beloved and the hero and the series as well. Not a chance.

Hardly a chance. There was one notorious exception. He first appeared in *Black Mask* during the early 1920's. His name was Race Williams, the first of the hardboiled detectives.

Few characters in mystery adventure fiction shared Williams' penchant for killing. It was always in self defense, but there never lived a man who had to defend himself more frequently.

Only slowly did the idea take hold that a hero might shoot someone dead (in a mystery story) and still not be transformed into a depraved fiend who had to be punished in the final paragraph. The idea crept by degrees through *Black Mask*, as years earlier it had entered the fiction of *Adventure, Complete Stories, Action Stories, Wild West Weekly*.

Eventually, the good guy with the flaming gun crossed over to *Detective Fiction Weekly*. Then other magazines featured him. In *Scotland Yard*, Detective Curt Flagg--an almost brainless behemoth--battered through prodigies of slaughter. In *Detective Dragnet* (later *10 Detective Aces*), Wade Hammond experienced a monthly crimson shambles. And various lead characters strewed *Clues* with endless bodies.

These deadly revels even breached the defenses of *Detective Story Magazine*, that bastion of curious propriety where heroes could rob, cheat, swindle, and deceive, but could never, never shoot to kill.

One day, as the 1930's glided up all around, it was suddenly no longer a social error for the hero to slay.

Suddenly, lethal heroes strode through every mystery magazine.

Murder by lead character had become acceptable, and the fiction filled with gore. The true, high-violence story packed pulp pages. After years of timid fussing, the detective now used his gun with deadly intent through stories strenuous and odd, written with Roman candles.

To those of you who rode through city streets to your local Steve's Magazine Exchange, these influences, delicately interlacing magazines and characters back through the decades, were dimly distant as Xiccarph.

What had you to do with that remote past when, for the first time, Race Williams blasted evil and the Continental Op sought solutions in shabby streets?

Your heart lay in the living present. In your fingers, the six magazines felt wonderfully firm, the covers smooth, the coarse paper emitting a scent deliciously woody. And concealed inside, behind the waiting paragraphs, guns beat and action throbbed and the hero was magnificent, indeed he was.

Read, and the hot adventure dissolved the thin stuff of your own life. The adventure possessed you utterly. You read netted in a web of passion and blood, indifferent to the past.

What price origins? At Steve's, dozens of additional magazines waited to be read.

The store was packed with them.

They had always been there. They always would be.

(Continued from page 2)
As it stands, Ray met a tragic and untimely demise in Texas, and of course my dear friend Mae succumbed in November, 1980.

The script of *Daddy Was a Lady* died with them.

(Continued from page 4) ponent is still ignorant of the doings of the Murderer until the old Opium Woman comes to his cell and reveals everything to him. He then commits suicide.

Forsyte's reconstruction of Jasper and his circumstances are entertainingly written, and, while I do not agree with much of it, I should state that the book is by no means a nut book (like so much other Droodism), but a doubtful, controversial book. I cannot say much in praise of Forsyte's routine continuation of the novel, though. Forsyte states frankly that he is not trying to write in Dickens' style, and that his material is compressed to about half the length that Dickens would have written. It is true that Forsyte deserves some credit for not trying to ape Dickens, but the result still seems like "The Unfinished Symphony" as finished by John Philip Sousa.

(Continued from page 1) Green, OH 43403), it can be had in paper for $10.95 or between hard covers for $15.95. I have not seen a copy of the book, but I did hear Ely speak about it at the last Popular Culture Association meeting and it sounds as though it would delight both the casual Sherlockian and his more fanatical brother.

Barry Van Tilburg's serial article on Spy Series Characters has been squeezed out of the last few issues, the victim of a lack of space, but it will be back, have no fear.

It's subscription-renewal time, the happiest time of the year for me, when I ask you folks to come up with twelve bucks apiece to keep me rolling in luxury here in the fun capital of the midwest. I'm enclosing an order blank for your convenience which you can also use to order copies of back issues as well as copies of the hardbound, facsimile edition of volume one of *The Armchair Detective*. *(Continued on page 32)*

IT'S ABOUT CRIME
by Marvin Lachman

NOTES ON RECENT READING

While Ngaio Marsh was dying, Jove Books was busy keeping her alive. They have been reprinting virtually all of her books, and it is now possible for the reader to trace her long career from its beginning, with *A Man Lay Dead* (1934), to her latest in paperback, *Photo Finish* (1980). One book remains to be published, posthumously, this fall [*Light Thickens*, Little, Brown, 15 October 1982, $13.95]. Like her contemporaries Sayers and Allingham, Marsh used elements of the thriller in her early work. *A Man Lay Dead*, though a detective story, is also about Bolsheviks, spies, and maidens in distress. It moves at a far crisper pace than later Marsh because there are fewer long passages detailing the interrogation of suspects.

If Marsh had a weakness, it was that her hero, Roderick Alleyn, spent too much time asking questions. More than compensating was her use of unusual murder methods. I can think of few authors as imaginative in how they disposed of victims-to-be. My favorite is the gun-in-the-piano in *Overture to Death* (1939), but there are other contenders; e.g., the wool-compressing machine in *Died in the Wool* (1945) and the swinging champagne bottle in *Vintage Murder* (1937).

Another Marsh strength was what Howard Haycraft dubbed the "Marsh-milieu." It was a world of artists, theater people, aristocracy, and civilized policemen. Far removed from the usual settings for murder in real life, it was all the better for escape reading because of that. Especially attractive were such theater novels as *Night at the Vulcan* (1951) and *Killer Dolphin* (1966). Not only did she make the people come alive, but she made you feel you were physically inside the theater.

Generally, Marsh's novels did not change too much from the classic detective type she used in her second, *Enter a Murderer* (1935). She returned to the thriller once, with excellent results, in *Spinsters in Jeopardy* (1953). Her attempts to modernize her books, by using the drug scene in *When in Rome* (1970), the leader of an emerging African nation in *Black as He's Painted* (1974), or the Mafia in *Photo Finish*, were not fully successful. Yet, each of these books contained enough traditional Marsh to satisfy her fans.

If I had a gun to my head and had to select only two Marsh books to recommend, I would pick *Overture to Death* and *Death in a White Tie* (1938). However, there are almost thirty others which I've read, enjoyed, and can recommend. Most are now available. Thank you, Jove.

Just as civilized as Dame Ngaio, but using a vastly different setting, are the two women who write as Emma Lathen. The many faces of the financial world are *their* milieu as they describe the cases of John Putnam Thatcher, vice president of the Sloan Bank. Pocket Books has just published their latest, *Go for the Gold* (1981), a book clearly inspired by the financing of the 1980 Winter Olympics in Lake Placid. They are also reprinting some of the earlier Lathen, and that is good news indeed. Especially, look for *Death Shall Overcome* (1966), out of print in paperback for over a decade. It's about the civil rights movement and an attempt to integrate Wall Street. It's a well-plotted mystery with a hilarious ending. Almost as good are *Pick Up Sticks* (1970), an ecologically sound mystery about murder along the Appalachian Trail, and *Ashes to Ashes* (1971), with the unusual background of a parochial school in Queens, New York City. The Lathen books are all fun, well written, and, incidentally, impart some knowledge about financial matters.

If four-letter words turn you off, avoid L.A. Morse. In any case, avoid his second book, *The Big Enchilada* (1982), which has nothing to recommend it. But, if you don't mind a lot of scatology and want to read the most unusual private-eye novel in years, I strongly suggest *The Old Dick* (Avon, 1981). This Edgar-winning paperback original is about 78-year-old Jake Spanner, a detective with a great line of patter who, though long retired, gets involved in "one more case" and finds his vital juices flowing again, literally and figuratively. It's a funny, fast-moving, violent book that says some things that need to be said about growing old in America in the 1980's. Incidentally, rumor has it that George Burns will play Spanner in a film version of *The Old Dick*. Poor casting; Art Carney would be better.

You'll find no four-letter words in the classics of detective fiction, but they, in their own way, are as readable as Morse. For example, try some of the books in Dell's outstanding MURDER INK/SCENE OF THE CRIME series. Raymond Chandler once savaged A.A. Milne's *Red House Mystery* (1922). He should have known better. This is a delightful mystery, different but as much fun in its adult way as that author's Winnie the Pooh books. Dell has also reprinted two of the best from Anthony Berkeley. Fifty years have not dulled the appeal of *The Poisoned Chocolates Mystery* (1929), with its intellectually satisfying multiple solutions. Even better is the same author's *Trial and Error* (1937), a book that starts with an intriguing premis: you only have six months to live and decide that before you die you will rid the world of someone who doesn't deserve to live. The complications that ensue make for one of the most original mysteries of the Golden Age.

Dell does not limit itself to the books of the twenties and thirties. Its two series, in fact, are replete with recent British mysteries. One of the most unusual of these is Leslie Thomas's *Dangerous Davies, the Last Detective* (1976), in which the klutziest, unluckiest British policeman compulsively investigates a 25-year-old disappearance. This is a book which, while not fully satisfying, is interesting and unusual enough for me to call it to your attention and to want to read other books by Thomas.

Surprisingly, some of the *real* classics of crime literature (I mean books written more than a century ago) are still readable. Take the usual attractive editions from Dover of works by the founding father and mother of the mystery novel, Wilkie Collins and Anna Katharine Green. Collins' *Moonstone* is a long, intricately plotted work of an author who came up with most of the devices in the field that Poe did not invent. Old fashioned, yes, but as enthralling as it was in 1868. Green is not as good a writer as Collins, and *The Leavenworth Case* (1878), often called the first American mystery novel, creaks a bit with old age. Yet, Green's New York City is interesting. Her sleuth, Ebenezer Gryce, is, as his name implies, not a very hard-boiled type, but he's not only one of the very first fictional detectives, he's also a good one.

Jon Breen quoted, for all readers of EQMM, my advice regarding avoidance of books with swastikas on their covers. At the risk of judging books by their covers, I also suggest you stay away from those with the United States presidential seal similarly displayed. I have read literally dozens of mysteries having to do with presidents, and almost all are bad. The worst seem to display the seal. A case in point is *Giant Killer* (1981), by Tom Hyman, recently reprinted by Bantam; it appeals neither to heart nor to mind, but goes right for the crotch. There is gratuitous sex and violence but no plausibility in this number about a trigger-happy U.S. president ready to take over Mexico. Caveat: empty book.

While I'm at it, I might as well mention that most books with flags on their covers leave a lot to be desired. Sean Flannery's *Hollow Men* (Charter, 1982) uses Israeli, Swiss, and U.N. flags, and it is not only hard to believe, it is not nearly as interesting as what is really happening in the area in which it is set, the Middle East. It seems to me that many writers, editors, and publishers have a badly mistaken idea of what readers are looking for in the way of escape. There are many problems in the workd, and if we are going to do our share toward solving them we should gather the facts by reading non-fiction so we can be intelligent citizens/voters. However, that time which I allot to "escape" reading is usually wasted for me if it only involves a fictional treatment of the same problems which I am trying to escape. Give me the private-eye novel or the weekend house party with the body in the library for my escape.

Yet there are exceptions, and I am glad I did not avoid Hardiman Scott's *Operation Ten* (a Cornelia and Michael Bessie book published by Harper & Row at $12.95) since it carries the Union Jack on its cover. However, one chapter convinced me this would be a "good read" and one of the rare examples of worthwhile fiction regarding terrorists. Four IRA fanatics plan to kidnap British Prime Minister Margaret Thatcher and hold her until England agrees to leave Northern Ireland. Wherefore is this unlikely plot better than all other unlikely plots? Scott avoids flashbacks and unnecessary description, simply carrying the reader along with the skill of his narrative drive.

Just what is the mystique that causes chronologically grown men and women to go ga-ga over paperback covers? I can't explain it, though I'm stricken with the disease myself. There must be a lot of us around, since the third book on the subject in a year has just been published as a trade paperback by Penguin for $12.95. Thomas L. Bonn's *Under Cover* is a good general survey of the subject, though there is not too much new information, I suspect, for readers of this column. For example, the section on future paperback collectables, which could have been very useful, is far too brief. Still, the reproductions are excellent, and they go beyond the usual arbitrary 1959 cut-off. They also demonstrate how much better paperback art used to be. This is a good coffee-table book, and I don't mean that in the pejorative sense. After you've read the text, you will find yourself opening it many times to look at the illustrations again.

Ernest Savage's *Two if by Sea* (Scribner's, $12.95) is Blake's *The Beast Must Die* told forty-five years later by an equally good writer. Both, though very different, tell of men seeking revenge for the hit-and-run automobile deaths of loved ones. There is detection in *Two if by Sea*, but it is minimal. The book's strong points are its buildup of suspense and Savage's razor-sharp dialogue. Also noteworthy is the setting, a freighter with luxury accomodations, sailing between Geneva and Seattle and carrying, in addition to the avenger and his prey, an assortment of interesting people. Only Savage's ending, though not bad, is not up to the rest of a very strong candidate for an Edgar nomination.

Speaking of Nicholas Blake, I recently caught up with his first mystery, *A Question of Proof* (1935, reprinted by Harper's Perennial Library). The setting, like many English first mysteries, is academic, and Blake used his experience as a schoolmaster, limning very well both schoolboys and teachers. The puzzle is a good one, worthy of the introduction of Blake's series sleuth, Nigel Strangeways. Nigel is a member of the silly-ass school of detection, though, like his colleagues, Messrs. Campion, Wimsey, and Queen, he grew more serious as he grew older. Also, Blake, in the future, was to generally avoid the one device that does not work in *A Question of Proof*: the author writing the book as if he were confiding in the reader. At one point, Blake even explicitly tells the reader that he is using a metaphor.

NOTES ON FUTURE READING: A PREDICTION

As I write this, some writer, inspired by the Tylenol deaths, is busily writing a mystery novel or short story having to do with a mass murderer who inserts poison into the ingredients of a product found on the shelves of many stores. It will be published within the year and will appeal to the same people who read books about earthquakes, skyscraper fires, assassinations, etc. I will probably not enjoy it. I hope the author will use English better than Illinois Attorney General Tyrone Fahner, who, shortly after the tragedy, was quoted as saying, redundantly, that the killings were the work of a "crazed madman." Fahner also said, "We're trying to understand what kind of person would do this kind of random thing--randomly pass out death ... to a child, a family, a stewardess."

(Continued on page 49)

REEL MURDERS
MOVIE REVIEWS by Walter Albert

FILM ILLUSIONISTS: MÉLIÈS, BROWNING, AND CLOUZOT

One of the "givens" of film history is that French director Georges Méliès, a magician who turned his talents from stage to film enchantments, is one of the great film innovators. In my surveys of French films, I have always dutifully shown Méliès' *Trip to the Moon* (1902) and talked glibly of the importance of his work. I was only repeating standard film history, and I had no real basis for believing it until this past weekend when I attended an extraordinary event sponsored by the film section of Pittsburgh's Carnegie Institute.

Méliès' granddaughter, Madeleine Malthète-Méliès, came to Pittsburgh to present three different programs of his films with piano accompaniment by Eric Leguen. I was able to see thirty-one of the forty-seven films she screened, including four that were hand-tinted, and what I saw on those two rainy, chilly October evenings was a revelation.

In the dozen years from about 1898 to 1910 that Méliès was producing and directing, he made over five hundred short films. His family has been able to assemble and restore only about 150, so the series we were shown represents about one third of the surviving films. Working before the era of the feature-length films that were to dominate world production after 1912, Méliès drew on his experience as a stage illusionist and his incomparable visual imagination. Disguises and transformations abound in his films, and he devised the dissolve, fade, and superimposed image to make his fantastic tricks possible. The prints are not always properly defined, and some of them are not complete, but the witty inventions from his apparently inexhaustible box of illusions are still a delight.

What is particularly striking about Méliès' films is their pacing, a perfectly choreographed comic rhythm that is at its most impressive when Méliès himself is performing. For director-producer-writer Méliès was also a comic actor of rare skill, with a good-natured pleasure in fooling an audience that is still infectious after eighty years. He was very fond of playing the role of the Devil, and the final film of the series, *Satan in Prison* (1907), was a perfect capstone to the screenings. In this dazzling film, the Devil-Méliès furnishes a bare cell out of his cape, complete to a lovely lady toasted at a candlelight midnight supper. When they are surprised by her jealous husband, she collapses into a heap of crumpled fabric in one of the most magical of Méliès' effects. Then, in a furious reverse movement, the Devil strips the room and, disappearing behind the cape, leaps toward the rear wall where the cape suddenly hangs suspended from two nails and, when it is pulled down, exposes a bare wall.

I mentioned to Madame Malthête-Méliès my pleasure in her grandfather's good humour, and she replied--her entire face lighting up--that even after he had lost everything else, he never lost his humour and was always playing the prankster, pulling innumerable cigarettes out of her ear. In his last years (he died in 1938), Méliès operated a toy shop in one of the Parisian train stations, but what I find most painful is the anecdote of the evening that Méliès burned all of his negatives in the garden of his Montreuil home. Fortunately, prints have survived, but those wasted years when he was eclipsed by a generation of gifted comedians--all of whom drew on his routines and inventions--is, I think, one of the great tragedies of film history.

Méliès' films may be thought of as marginal to films of mystery and detection, but not if one remembers the many writers and directors of mystery films who have either been accomplished magicians or interested in magic and who have made use of this in their films.

Tod Browning was a director who used theatrical illusion in several of his best films, and the rarely seen *Miracles for Sale* (MGM, 1939), based on Clayton Rawson's *Death from a Top Hat*, makes extensive use of magic in a suspenseful melodrama of stage magicians and psychic phenomena. Robert Young does a competent job as Michael Morgan, a re-named Rawson Merlini, who has unaccountably acquired a folksy father played by Frank Craven in his best *Our Town* style. (I wonder if MGM didn't entertain some faint hope that this film might spawn a series with Young/Craven sharing in some of the popularity of the Ellery Queen father-son duo.) It's a well-produced film in which Morgan, through damsel-in-distress Judy Barkley (played by Florence Rice), becomes involved in spiritualism and murder, but the spookiness of the premise is undercut by some conventional thirties' farce. There is a seance that has some of the style--and chills--of Browning's better work, and fanciers of such things will be interested to see Gloria Holden (the daughter of the underrated *Dracula's Daughter*) in another of her frozen-face roles but with none of the sexual perversity that made her playing in the earlier film more interesting. *Miracles for Sale* comes off as a glossy, entertaining swan song for Browning, and it is unfortunate that most people now know his work through *Dracula*, which is his least characteristic film and far from his best. You will not find in *Miracles for Sale* the brilliance of *Freaks* (with its superb bridal party sequence), but it's an accomplished bit of directing and should not be relegated to a footnote in a history of his career.

Since I seem to be in a retrospective mood, I will recommend as the best thriller of my recent experience a French film you're not likely to see at your neighborhood theater or on late-night TV. It's Henri-Georges Clouzot's *Le Corbeau* (*The Raven*), financed by a German producing company and released in occupied France in 1943. Movie-goers whose memories go back to the fifties may remember the great success of two of Clouzot's films on the art-house circuit, *The Wages of Fear*

A QUARTERLY JOURNAL DEVOTED TO THE APPRECIATION
OF
MYSTERY, DETECTIVE AND SUSPENSE FICTION

Volume 1 Number 1
October 1967

At last, after fourteen years, the first volume of *The Armchair Detective* is again in print.

When Allen J. Hubin published volume one, number one, back in October 1967, he ran off only a few hundred copies. As more and more people discovered TAD, the inevitable clamor for back issues arose and the volume was quickly out of print. Those lucky enough to have copies generally hung on to them tightly, and the occasional copies that *did* come up for sale were snapped up before the ink on their price tags had time to dry.

Now that's changed. No longer must one have good luck and a tidy sum of money to pick up a copy of TAD volume one. The first volume of TAD is now available, in a quality, clothbound, facsimile edition, for the cost of a current subscription to TAD (plus $1.00 for postage and handling).

In addition to the original 158 pages of volume one — which included contributions by such luminaries as William S. Baring-Gould, James Keddie, Jr., J. R. Christopher, William K. Everson, Charles Shibuk, Marvin Lachman, Norman Donaldson, James Sandoe, Ordean Hagen, Jon L. Breen, Nigel Morland, and Francis M. Nevins, Jr. — this edition contains a specially written introduction by TAD's founder and long-time editor, Al Hubin.

The volume is Smyth sewn, casebound, and printed on fifty pound Finch Opaque paper. The page size is 8½" x 11", same as the original, though a slight reduction in the size of the printing has been made to provide room for binding.

For each book, send a check (made payable to Brownstone Books) for $17.00 ($16.00 plus $1.00 for postage and handling) to:

Brownstone Books
**1711 Clifty Dr.
Madison, Indiana 47250**

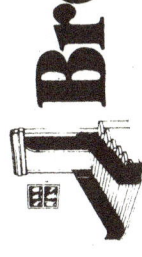

RENEWAL FORM

PLEASE REMOVE AND RETURN WITH YOUR CHECK

[ ] Volume 6, complete, $12.00*

[ ] *The Armchair Detective*, Volume One. A quality, hardbound, facsimile edition of the first four numbers of the premier mystery magazine. Includes all 158 pages of the original 1967-1968 issues in an 8½ x 11" format, plus a four-page introduction written especially for this edition by TAD's founder and long-time editor, Al Hubin. $17.00.

Mail to: Guy M. Townsend
        1711 Clifty Drive
        Madison, IN 47250

_____
(Name)

_____
(Address)

_____
(City, State)   (Zip Code)

---

[1] The first seven issues of TMF have been reprinted in a 5½ x 8½" format uniform with the current TMFs (originally, the first four of these were printed in an 8½ x 11" format). NOTE: These are *reprints*, not originals.

[2] Only a few copies left, and they are missing covers. The contents, however, are complete.

[3] Only a few copies left.

[4] Volume 6, number 2, is in short supply; when they are gone the remaining individual issues of volume six will be sold at $2.50 apiece.

RENEWAL FORM

PLEASE REMOVE AND RETURN WITH YOUR CHECK

RENEWAL SPECIAL

Renew your subscription to TMF before the first of the year and you may also purchase a new, *signed* copy of Joe L. Hensley's latest Don Robak novel, *Outcasts* (Doubleday, 1981), for only $5.95, postpaid. That's four dollars less than list price.

Please put a check before the items you are ordering

[ ] *The Mystery Fancier*, volume seven (1983), domestic second-class, $12.00
[ ] *The Mystery Fancier*, volume seven (1983), first class, U.S. & Canada, $15.00
[ ] *The Mystery Fancier*, volume seven (1983), overseas surface rate, $12.00
[ ] *The Mystery Fancier*, volume seven (1983), overseas air mail, $18.00

[ ] Joe L. Hensley, *Outcasts*, $5.95 (with renewals before 31 December)

TMF BACK ISSUES

[ ] Volume One, plus Preview Issue, $20.00[1]
[ ] Volume 2, number 3, $2.50[2]
[ ] Volume 2, number 4, $2.50
[ ] Volume 2, number 6, $2.50[3]
[ ] Volume 3, number 2, $2.50
[ ] Volume 3, number 3, $2.50
[ ] Volume 3, number 4, $2.50

[ ] Volume 3, number 5, $2.50
[ ] Volume 4, complete, $12.00
[ ] Volume 3, number 6, $2.50
[ ] Volume 5, number 1, $2.50
[ ] Volume 5, number 2, $2.50
[ ] Volume 5, number 6, $2.50

Good News for TADians!

Volume one of *The Armchair Detective*, long out of print, is now available in a hardbound, facsimile edition.

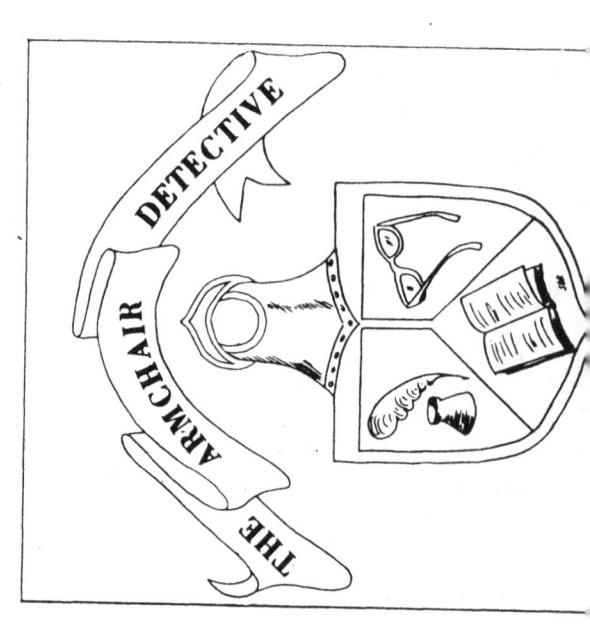

(1953) and *Diaboliques* (1955), the latter with its unforgettable body-in-the-bathtub scene.

Clouzot's reputation had already been established in France with three films: *The Murderer Lives at No. 21* (1942), based on a novel by Belgian writer André Steeman; *Le Corbeau*; and, one of my other favorites, *Quai des Orfevres* (1947), released in this country as *Jenny Lamour* and with a fine cast headed by Louis Jouvet, one of France's legendary actor-directors.

Le Corbeau was originally conceived by writer Louis Chavance in 1937 (effectively taking care of the later charge that the film was written to put the French in the worst possible light) and was based on an incident involving the writing of poison-pen letters in Marseilles. In Clouzot's film, the anecdote which serves as the basic narrative thread is only a pretext to allow him to film a pessimistic study of provincial life in which everyone is hiding something and is a likely suspect for the writer who signs himself as "le Corbeau." The initial letters expose a relationship between an idealistic doctor, Rémy Germain (played by Pierre Fresnay) and the wife of his respected elder colleague, psychiatrist Dr. Vorzet, but before the movie reaches its disturbing conclusion 850 letters have indicted what appears to be just about everybody of any importance in St. Robin.

Clouzot has been compared to Hitchcock in his ability to play skillfully on the spectators' nerves, but Clouzot has none of the wit of the British filmmaker, and the town seems to be tainted by a slow rot that even the exposure of the identity of the Raven will not remove. (*Shadow of a Doubt* is closest in tone to *Le Corbeau*, but the basic goodness of at least some of Hitchcock's characters does not become suspect.) With his camera menacing every character's movements, shadows mimic the black bird's shape until, at the end, a veiled avenger, clothed in white, is costumed and photographed as a mocking parody of the bird of death.

Two sequences deserve special note: a funeral cortege for the victim of the poison-pen letters, with superbly detailed close-ups of the townspeople silently watching the procession as the mourners step over and around a letter that has fallen from the hearse; and the flight of the chief suspect down empty streets invaded by the threatening shouts of an unseen mob, growing in intensity until glass shatters in her room where she has taken refuge and forces her to rush out into the arms of waiting authorities. And, in a scene which serves as a key to Clouzot's intentions, the investigator-psychiatrist Vorzet uses a slowly swinging lamp to demonstrate to Dr. Germain our ambivalent demonic/angelic nature in a relentless alternating of light and shadow that is ironically descriptive of the director's nightmare vision.

Méliès, Browning, Clouzot: their methods may differ and they are not similar stylistically, but they are all accomplished directors who use the camera to deceive and mystify audiences. Méliès may be the first and, perhaps, the best of film magicians, but this marvelous theater of illusions that is film has many rooms, and who knows what delightful or terrifying furnishings we shall find behind the next door we open?

MYSTERY·FILE Short Reviews by Steve Lewis

Erle Stanley Gardner. *The Case of the Perjured Parrot*. Ballantine, 1982 (first published in 1939), 167 pp., $2.25.

    The problem, of course, with the Perry Mason stories is that the characters are totally flat and one-dimensional. Gardner's prose, utilitarian at best, is designed only to tell the story and is best otherwise ignored.
    But the stories he tells--I can't resist 'em. They're low on action and high in idea content. The plot and red herrings are simply mind-dazzling--if only you could sort them out!
    I read one chapter and I'm hooked. I've guessed who done it from time to time, but not very often. I read too fast, I think, and Mason's too smart for me.
    Gardner is obsessed with circumstantial evidence, and it helps to keep in mind that his facts are always subject to considerable variation. This time I thought I'd outguessed him, but somehow he managed to zig left just as I was zagging right.
    Involved are at least three parrots, hints of police graft and corruption, forged checks, multi-bigamous marriages and questionable divorce decrees, a will and two widows, and a time of death that turns out to be of utmost importance.
    Mason also makes an ass out of another pompous witness. You'd think they'd learn. (B)

Jonathan Valin. *Dead Letter*. Dodd, Mead, 1981, 248 pp., $9.95.

    The key to this, the third adventure of Cincinnati private eye Harry Stoner, is academia, and the scurrilous sort of infighting and back-stabbing that it is rumored goes on in such circles. As one of the characters puts it on page 197, "They don't make very good human beings, scholars. They don't have it in them to care for anything but themselves and their work."
    I could argue the point, I think, but hardly with 100 percent conviction. The fact remains that this case of Harry Stoner's is at once his most confusing and his most involving. Neither his client, a professor who believes his Marxist-environmentalist daughter has stolen a secret government document from him, nor the daughter herself are quite what Stoner takes them at first to be.
    Professor Daryl Lovingwell loves his daughter Sarah, or so

he says. After his death, Stoner discovers an immense hatred between the two, and yet, although he had liked his client, with Kate gone (the library cop Stoner had become so involved with in *Final Notice*), the inevitable begins to happen between Sarah and himself.

In a number of ways, this case is a tough one to fathom, and even more so for the reader. Characterizations are deliberately murky, sketched from a multitude of conflicting viewpoints. The entire affair is filled with a moral ambiguity almost unnatural for a detective story.

And so this is unlikely to be everyone's favorite Harry Stoner novel--there is not much here to brighten the overall gloom. If it should come to it, however, a second reading will reveal how tightly structured this tale actually is. While it may not have been totally visible the first time, above all what it will demonstrate is that as an author, Jonathan Valin knows exactly what it is that he's up to. (A minus)

Murray Sinclair. *Only in L.A.* A&W Publishers, 1982, 213 pp., $12.95.

A couple of books back [see *A Cracking of Spines* in TMF 6:5] I was talking about mood and atmosphere and their place in detective stories. Here's another, a broody melodrama with a problem that's very similar, although continents apart. In a way, *Only in L.A.* is a modern-day paean to life in the squalor of southern California, although from the outside "paean" would hardly seem to be the right word to use.

Consistency is not Sinclair's problem. He hits a single note on the very first page, and he holds it throughout the rest of the book, apparently without even straining. Both he and his hero, screenwriter Ben Crandel, view Los Angeles as the ultimate symbol of a dying culture at the end of its spiritual life-line. A citizens' group central to the plot attempts to make Hollywood the adult entertainment capital of the U.S., and foolishly so, as if it weren't already.

Crandel's first appearance was in *Tough Luck L.A.*, a paperback original from Pinnacle, and to say that the mystery involved, and its solution, were totally incomprehensible would be an act of utmost charity.

Sinclair has a much better hold on his story ling this time around, but only if you consider massive unexplained coincidence as the ultimate in plotting devices.

On the other hand, it occurs to me that perhaps we're meant only to consider it an indispensible part of the delirious madness and seedy, sour-tasting pornography that Crandel finds himself swallowed up by as he desperately tries to find his adopted son's kidnappers.

It's a point of view, and I'm sure it's a valid one. It's like spinach, though. You can sit and admire all its fine qualities all you want, and still be awfully glad you don't have to eat any. (C plus)

John D. MacDonald. *Cinnamon Skin*. Harper & Row, 1982, 275 pp., $13.95.

Coming out later this year, also from Harper & Row, is a

collection of some of the short stories John D. MacDonald did for the detective pulps back at the beginning of his career, in the late forties and early fifties. The title will be *The Good Old Stuff,* and I'm sure it will be, given some picking and choosing, but all things considered, JDM was only learning his trade at the time. Even given the loss of certain intangibles like youthful ambition and desire, the stuff he's writing today has to be considered light-years better than any that he wrote over thirty years ago, by any standards.

As anyone who has read *Free Fall in Crimson* could have easily predicted, it is Travis McGee's closest friend, Meyer, who is in dire need of rehabilitation at the beginning of *Cinnamon Skin,* the twentieth and latest in this best-selling series. McGee lives in a world of constant tragedy, and unfortunately that's what it takes to snap Meyer out of his year-long doldrums.

Blown out of the water in an ear-shattering explosion, purportedly set off by an unknown group of Chilean terrorists, is Meyer's boat, the *John Maynard Keynes*. (Meyer is a world-famous economist, as you may or may not be surprised to learn.) On board was Meyer's niece, his only living relative, and her new husband.

Readers familiar with life in McGee's universe will suspect that all is not what it seems, even before the evidence starts coming in.

The murderer's trail leads to Texas and upstate New York before swooping back down to Mexico, where Meyer and McGee unite their efforts with those of a modern-day Mayan princess in obtaining a final bit of retribution. Their prey is a lady-killer of some duration, who promises not to yield without an all-out struggle.

Most of the action will be found in these final few chapters. Those seeking an epic saga crammed with rugged blood-and-guts action and suspense will have to look elsewhere. This is a detective story, pure and simple, albeit with a dash more of relentless vigilantism than you'd expect in a more law-abiding sort of adventure.

As if to compensate for the lack of action in the early going, boiled away as it were in the intense Texas sun, there is enough reflective and introspective interaction and byplay between the characters to more than maintain MacDonald's reputation as America's number one philosophical myth-master and debunker. JDM often puts into words what the rest of us only feel.

In spite of being today the object of almost constant academic scrutiny, MacDonald has added another fine entry to his cumulative bibliography. While there is a definite feeling of *deja vu* closing in over the horizon, as if some elements and patterns in his work are beginning to constantly repeat themselves, John D. MacDonald is still a slick, effective writer. Even if much of the crude vitality of his younger days is gone, the keen, sharp insights he has into each of his characters are still more than sufficient to meet any challenge presented to them. (B plus)

Stephen Greenleaf. *Death Bed.* Ballantine, 1982 (first published in hardcover in 1980), 232 pp., $2.50.

If you're a private eye fan and you haven't yet discovered Stephen Greenleaf, then you've been missing one of the bright new names in the field. This is only his second book, and already, for all intents and purposes, he has the formula down to perfection.

Greenleaf's detective is an ex-lawyer named John Marshall Tanner. The scene is San Francisco, home of more private detectives per capita than any other city in the nation, Los Angeles notwithstanding. Tanner's client is a rich man who is dying of cancer and who wants his alienated son found. Tanner is hired to find him.

The son, however, is a leftover radical from the stormy Brekeley days of the sixties. He is also wanted by the police. The amount of money he would inherit is sizable, and naturally there are those who would also like their hands on it, which they would were Tanner to fail.

Tanner also has other irons in the fire. A crusading reporter who prefers to work incognito has come up missing, and the police are worried about an unknown underground organization rumored to be buying up all the guns and ammunition on the black market that they can. Tanner has to do some fancy footwork just to remember what case he's working on at what time.

I mentioned "formula" above. As any experienced PI enthusiast will immediately recognize, all these cases that Tanner finds himself working on are not separate, but one. As far as PI fans are concerned, however, the more complex the plot is, the happier they are, and Greenleaf has enough twists involved in this labyrinthic maze of conflicting emotions and desires to satisfy anyone's cravings.

The combination of mood and atmosphere is black: dark, ugly, and violent. The writing is solid--if anything, perhaps a little too solid. Take this passage from page 202, for example. It's fairly typical: "Five cups of coffee and three hotcakes later I was on the road, a counter-commuter driving in the opposite direction from the rush-hour throng of East Bay businessmen and Christmas shoppers, plunging headlong into the rising sun and into the past of a family who undoubtedly preferred to forget it."

It's a well-written, picturesque paragraph-sentence, but it's not one entirely conducive to speed-reading. It runs-- if you'll forgive me--counter-commuter-wise to the flow of the story, if you see what I mean.

All the ingredients of a successful private eye series are here. For my own part, I wish I didn't have this underlying feeling that everything--what have you: the mood, the complex plot, the overly elaborate set of metaphors and similies-- wasn't just a trifle *too* calculated.

Which is to say, if only I could get it into words, I continually felt as though I were being forced to admire all the great scenery going by--without ever being able to sit back and enjoy the ride. (B plus)

Jessica Mann. *Funeral Sites*. Doubleday/Crime Club, 1982 (first published in 1981), 186 pp., $10.95.

Books can fool you sometimes. (I seldom read dust jackets. They give too much away.) Take this one, for example. It starts out as just another murder mystery, but before you can whisper Hercule Poirot it's turned into something else altogether.

Suspicious of the circumstances surrounding the death of her sister, the daughter of a former British prime minister suddenly finds the stakes higher than she or anyone could ever have imagined. Her sister's husband intends to become the next prime minister, and he refuses to let anyone stand in his way. Woe to anyone left alive with a working knowledge of his Cambridge past!

In this suddenly burgeoning conspiracy to take over the entire British government there are even hints that the Russians are involved. Quite naturally, this is the sort of story that would strike harder home over in England, where it was first published, but still, even here on this side of the Atlantic, there are some unexpected twists in store.

The book's too short to be truly convincing--in looking back I don't think I really believed a word of it for more than a minute--but in a number of ways what this also turns out to be is an engagingly entertaining feminist's version of John Buchan's *Thirty-nine Steps*. (Which, of course, is the all-time British spy-adventure classic that, one way or another, is always used as a basis for comparison when anything remotely similar comes along.) (B minus)

George Harmon Coxe. *The Camera Clue*. Dell, 1937, 192 pp.

Another feature of these old Dell mapbacks, besides the obvious one, of course, is the listing of the cast of characters, even before the title page. The map didn't help much with the mystery this time, but it is interesting to note that of the twenty characters listed, at least nine of them are on the scene outside the murdered man's office when Kent Murdock stops to take a candid shot of a sandwich advertising man on stilts.

Most of them don't want their picture taken, either. Murdock's office soon begins to resemble Grand Central Station, with worried people continually running in and out, desperately trying to keep him from publishing it in the newspaper. Murdock's assistant, Gowan, even gets his skull crushed in, by someone even more desperate than the others.

This was George Harmon Coxe's third novel--Kent Murdock is still definitely married, and whatever became of Joyce Murdock anyway? Formerly a writer for *Black Mask* and the other detective pulps of the twenties and thirties, Coxe was never known as a great wordsmith, and his massive total of camera-oriented plots soon became rather repetitious.

He was a pretty good master of misdirection, however, and here's a fine example of how he played the game of "fool the reader" so well. The big climax misfires just slightly, but even so I have to admit I was caught off-balance by its outcome, exactly as I was supposed to be. In one sense I wasn't even close, and I am chagrined to say I should have been.

And no, the sandwich man didn't do it. (C plus)

Stephen Greenleaf. *State's Evidence*. Dial Press, 1982, 310 pp., $15.95.

A few books back, as you may recall, I had some misgivings about *Death Bed*, Stephen Greenleaf's tale of private eye John Marshall Tanner that immediately preceded this one.
Ignore all that. Please. If you're a fan of PI fiction at all, whatever you do, don't let this one pass you by!

Toned down, but thankfully never quite eliminated, is some of the overbearing narrative that has marked Greenleaf's two earlier books. The dialogue now carries a greater share of the story, and the plotline is far less reliant on the flowery but not always appropriate series of metaphors that Greenleaf seemed to put so much stake in before.

It all begins when Tanner is hired by a deputy district attorney in the town of El Gordo to find a missing witness, a woman who claims to have seen a fatal hit-and-run accident.

But--do you remember ever watching the TV series *The Outsider*? El Gordo is one of those typically Californian towns that private eyes keep stumbling across, bright and sunny on the surface, but simply riddled with hostility, crime, and corruption just underneath.

It doesn't take Tanner long to start digging, nor for the foul matter to start making itself known.

Naturally, not all is what it seems. Some of the missing woman's friends believe that she's been kidnapped, murdered, or worse. Others feel she has merely fled her husband, a quietly arrogant tyrant with a fetish for things Oriental.

Surprisingly, everyone who has known the woman reveals to Tanner a completely different side to her personality. Not surprisingly, little by little, Tanner is forced to realize that D.A. Tolson has not told him all he needs to know about the case. Even the federal government, it seems, is vitally interested in its outcome.

Rampant coincidence seems to abound, but in each instance there is a substantive reason behind each of the bombshells Tanner soon begins to uncover.

And bombshells they are. An added plus, at least so far as I was concerned, was the touch of courtroom theatrics à la Perry Mason that highlights a central portion of the book. Tanner is also an ex-lawyer, and it's about time we saw that fact become a more essential part of one of his cases.

It may not happen, but Greenleaf should begin to start getting the recognition he deserves with this book. It's certainly fine enough to suggest that he's beginning to nudge his way out from behind the shadows of Chandler and Macdonald--his predecessors down these same dark alleys of Californian hypocrisy and despair. (A)

Cyril Hare. *The Wind Blows Death*. Perennial Library, 1982 (originally published as *When the Wind Blows* in 1949), 248 pp., $2.95.

In *A Catalogue of Crime*, Barzun and Taylor hail this as a masterpiece, certainly the best of Hare's mystery novels. Realizing that their basis for judgment is, was, and always will be how a book measures up as a *detective* story, it's easy to see how they came to such a conclusion.

It's a good book, but I have some complaints. Most of them may be completely personal, but, then again, what do you think?

For the moment, however, let's start this review over, from the beginning. According to what I deduce from page 84, this is the third case of murder that amateur detective Francis Pettigrew finds himself involved in. Here he is now as the honorary treasurer to the Markshire Orchestral Society. Murdered is the featured soloist for one of their performances, violinist Lucy Carless.

A good many curious circumstances surround the murder, many of them having a good deal to do with alibis, hampered by an abundance of semi-secret sexual dalliances of varying degrees of ardor. Helping Pettigrew sort it all through (although nominally it is the other way around) are an aggressive new inspector named Trimble and his rather more laid-back superior, Chief Constable MacWilliam.

The characterizations are fine--although in essence perhaps more reflective of stereotypes than actual personages-- and the plotting is ingenious. As I stated above, I'd like to raise a few objections, but if you haven't read the book, please use your own judgment before plunging on.

1) The solution is slightly unfair, in that while a knowledge of Dickens might help, a complete familiarity with matters orchestral is mandatory. Without it, you'll never solve the case.

2) Throughout the investigation very little discussion of the motive is made. Naturally, it's a key to the solution. Again, an obscure bit of English law is needed to substantiate the matter. Unfair, I say.

3) There is no satisfactory reason given as to why the killer felt so compelled to come up with such an elaborate plan for doing away with the victim, except, of course, the requirements of the story. (The more complicated the knot, the harder it is to undo.)

4) And this is the one that bothered me the most. Maybe you'll think nothing of it, but when Pettigrew and MacWilliam sit down and begin discussing the case on page 186, all of a sudden the reader is left out of their deliberations. Here's where I was pulled up short and forcibly reminded--not unlike being hit over the head with a blunt instrument--that this is, after all, nothing more than a detective story, and we're only playing a game.

5) Which reminds me of my final point: Nobody, but nobody, ever expresses anything more than passing regret, if that, over the death of the victim.

Other than that, I liked the book fine. (B minus)

(Continued from page 18)

So far, all domestic subscriptions have been via second class mail, which, to be charitable, is a bit erratic in its delivery. For years Steve Stilwell has been after me to offer first-class mail service to those who wanted to foot the extra expense, and for years I've declined to do so, partly because I enjoy riling Steve almost as much as he enjoys riling me, but also because I doubted that there was anyone else out there who would be willing to pay extra to obtain more prompt and reliable delivery of his TMF. A couple of months ago, however, one of TMF's new subscribers telephoned for a chat and expressed a willingness to pay the freight to get his copy to him sooner. Now, two people doesn't exactly amount to a landslide, but there may be a few others out there who would

(Continued on page 39)

VERDICTS
More Reviews

Ellis Peters. *The Virgin in the Ice: The Sixth Chronicle of Brother Cadfael.* Macmillan, 1982, 220 pp.

Edith Mary Pargeter, who writes crime novels as Ellis Peters (and who has also produced short stories, translations, and non-crime novels, the latter published under her birth name), is once again back on familiar territory in *The Virgin in the Ice,* which follows *A Morbid Taste for Bones, One Corpse too Many, Monk's-Hood, Saint Peter's Fair,* and *The Leper of Saint Giles* in her series featuring Brother Cadfael, a twelfth-century Benedictine of the "fraternal house of Saint Peter and Saint Paul at Shrewsbury."

Brother Cadfael, who moves about with a good deal of freedom both within and without his monastery, is a former Crusader, now for many years a faithful, sincerely devout member of his order who specializes as herbalist and physician to his brotherhood. He is also, though he wouldn't claim the title, a detective.

In his current adventure, Cadfael bends efforts to save the life of one Brother Elyas, a Benedictine from the Worchester house, who has been almost fatally beaten and "hacked" by unknown assailants. The victim is being cared for at Bromfield Priory, and Brother Cadfael is summoned to care for him. His concern for the psychological and spiritual as well as the physical well-being of his patient leads the physician-monk-detective into the search for Elyas's missing charges, a brother and sister, Yves and Ermina Hugonin, and their further escort, a Benedictine nun, Sister Hilaria. The discovery of the raped and battered body of a young woman frozen into a streambed transforms the hunt into a search for a murderer as well.

These crimes and the subsequent disorders which flow from them are both effect and symbol of the general disorder which besets England in Brother Cadfael's times, for the country is in the grip of civil war, the throne the object of deadly contention between King Stephen and Empress Maud. Brother Cadfael is concerned but not despairing about England's winter of discontent:

> England was already frozen into a winter years long, and he knew it. King Stephen was crowned, and held, however slackly, most of England. The Empress Maud, his rival for the throne, held the west, and came with a claim the equal of Stephen's. Cousins,

> most uncousinly, they tore each other and tore England between
> them, and yet life must go on, faith must go on, the stubborn de-
> fiance of fortune must go on in the husbandry of the year, season
> after season, plough and harrow and seed, tillage and harvest.
> And here in the cloister and the church, the sowing and tillage
> and harvest of souls. Brother Cadfael had no fear for mankind,
> whatever became of mere men.... [A child expected in the town]
> would be a new generation, a new beginning, a new affirmation,
> spring in mid-winter. (p. 10)

Convincingly able to hate the sin and love the sinner, Brother Cadfael sets about restoring what order he can to his immediate environment, and he accomplishes a good deal: he finds a killer, takes on a band of particularly vicious marauders, nurtures a love affair, and cures souls. Peters/Pargeter also accomplishes quite a lot. She reveals further details of Brother Cadfael's colorful past; introduces us to a wide range of new characters; reports upon the progress of established characters, particularly Hugh and Aline Peringar; and makes the winter of 1139 vivid, immediate, and real.

Because this is a historical novel and because the central consciousness is Brother Cadfael's (though the story is told in the third person), Peters never points out the similarities between the unquiet twelfth century and the present day, but, of course, those similarities are in the reader's mind constantly; they are inescapable, and they certainly contribute to the immediacy. The Peters style in these novels, slightly reminiscent of early English poetry, also contributes to the vividness of her evocation of the Middle Ages, and the names help--spellings are archaic but perfectly apprehendable, and French names abound. But most important of all, perhaps, is Peters' careful rendering of the homely details--herbs, their uses, clothing, relationships of time and distance for a man on horseback, weaponry--these and a host of other minutiae lend force to the background until twelfth-century Britain becomes almost a character in the story.

All this goes on with no break or drag in the action, which is satisfying and compelling. Regular readers may well find a certain similarity in the resolution of this story to other series solutions, but this fact will in no way discourage them from accompanying Brother Cadfael upon future journeys, joining him in future efforts to shed a bit of light in his corner of the Dark Ages. (Jane S. Bakerman)

James Melville. *A Sort of Samurai*. St. Martin's Press, 1981, 168 pp., $9.95.

There is a bit of mystery surrounding *A Sort of Samurai*. It is the third in Melville's series of novels featuring Tetsuo Otani, Superintendent of the Hyogo Prefectural Police. The first two were *The Wages of Zen* (1979) and *The Chrysanthemum Chain* (1980). The mystery is that nowhere in or on this book is there any mention of their having been previous Otani books. The "about the author" paragraph makes no mention of them, and the publisher's remarks on the jacket flap state that with this book Melville "introduces the world" to Superintendent Otani.

On Saturday in Kobe at the end of the Golden Week holiday,

there is an earthquake of force seven on the Richter scale. Otani is on duty at Prefect Headquarters, and after the quake he takes a police car for a cruise around the city to scout damages. By a warehouse he hears a weird howling, investigates, and comes upon a peaceful, bloodless corpse in an office, accompanied by its baying pet Labrador. The immediate evidence points to death by heart attack, but an autopsy shows that the deceased, Richard Liebermann, died from a suspiciously strange cause--the cessation of blood flow through the carotid artery. Convinced that Liebermann, a German citizen, was probably murdered, Otani directs his two specialist detectives to help. Jiro Kimura, the flashy, self-styled Westernized playboy, specializes in cases involving Europeans, and it is he who interviews the other German employees of the warehouse. "Ninja" Noguchi specializes in gangland crime, narcotics, and crimes in slums and Korean ghettos; he is directed to follow leads which imply a pornography link to Liebermann. Otani happens to learn that a friend knows the victim and his wife, and so he investigates their background. The investigations of the three detectives take them to musty warehouse docks, *bunraku* puppet plays, and the homes of Japanese nobility.

Melville, himself a student of Japanese-language crime novels, has portrayed Kobe and certain slices of Japanese culture in a sharp, discerning, and interesting way. All of the important elements of the story involve things Japanese. The murder method is a mystery itself and turns out to be particularly Japanese. There are some clues from *Haiku* verses. Inspector Kimura's perception of Westerners is so acute that we see the idea of the "inscrutable Oriental" from the other side. Last but not least, the interplay between the characters, especially Otani and his men, has an inherent tenseness and formality that seems purely Japanese.

This is by far the best book of Melville's short series. The first book was an awkward combination of police story and espionage thriller. The second was needlessly marred by a narrative division throughout between Otani and a young British Vice-Consul who was given so much space that I thought he would become a Watson to Otani in future books. But *A Sort of Samurai* is a solid, well-constructed police procedural with a mysterious crime, a burning motive, fascinating characters, and some very fine ethnographic writing. (Greg Goode)

Geoffrey Bocca. *Best Seller: A Nostalgic Celebration of the Less-Than-Great Books You have Always Been Afraid to Admit You Loved.* Wyndham Books, 1981, 235 pp.

Of course, some of us haven't been afraid to admit we loved the books discussed in this volume by Geoffrey Bocca, but few of us have been able to discuss them with the verve and humor that he does here. I would love to list the complete table of contents, but I'll content myself with mentioning those chapters of special interest to mystery fans--the ones on *The Great Impersonation* and *Trent's Last Case*. would you believe that reading this book actually had me panting to read *The Great Impersonation*? Well, it did. I'd already read E.C. Bentley's classic, but Bocca's discussion of it made me realize that it was even better than I'd thought it was. And soon now I'm going to have to reread *King Solomon's Mines*, not to mention *The Virginian*. (Bocca quotes a paragraph from *The Virginian* that's almost as good as anything in F. Scott Fitzgerald.)

I see that I've strayed away from mysteries. Let's just say that there is also extensive discussion of some great adventure novels, some of which I've never read. I now feel a great void for having missed out on *The Scarlet Pimpernel* and *Under Two Flags*, as well as *Beverly of Graustark*. I feel, however, warmed by my own memories of *Beau Geste* and *Tarzan of the Apes*; it's a pleasure to see that Bocca loves them as much as I do. And he doesn't restrict himself to books. He's apparently seen every movie version ever made of all the books he likes, and he talks about them as well as he does the print versions. Bocca says that writing this book left him red-eyed and ill-humored. Reading it was a pure pleasure. I can't imagine anyone who's read any of the books he discusses not enjoying it. I recommend it highly. (Bill Crider)

Michael Gilbert. *End-Game*. Harper and Row, 1982.

If anyone questions whether Michael Gilbert is one of the most versatile mystery writers of out time, or whether he has a superb command of the techniques of the suspense story, *End-Game* should answer those questions for a long time to come. A glance at the titles of his recent books will confirm that he is willing to undertake a broad variety of types of stories, including professional espionage (*Mr. Calder and Mr. Behrens*), professional detection (*The Killing of Katie Steelstock*), amateur espionage (*The 92nd Tiger*), amateur detection (*The Family Tomb*), and the social-theme suspense novel (*Flash Point*). *End-Game* is a tale of professional detection, but one manifestation of Gilbert's mastery of the art of concealment lies in the fact that even the classification of the story is part of the mystery until four-fifths of the way through the book.

The theme of this novel is corrupt practices in business, with specific reference to the financial empire of Randall Blackett, a business tycoon whose operation is under covert observation by the police. Besides the regular police, who play a minor part in the story, the real protagonists are David Rhys-Morgan and Susan Perronet-Conde, whose status and motives are part of the mystery: Are they police, or private enquiry agents, or do they have some other, perhaps illicit, reasons for investigating Blackett's operation? Are they working together (as the reader will probably suspect), or are they alienated, as the writer leads us to believe? Thus we have a two pronged mystery, involving not only the question of whether the suspect is guilty, but also of who the villains are.

Gilbert has built this story around a figure, derived from the childhood game of "Snakes and Ladders," in which the player tries to work his way across the board by climbing the ladders and avoiding the danger of being snatched downward by the snakes. The figure of one of the protagonists climbing upward while the other climbs downward is stressed repeatedly to the extent that it becomes the dominant image of the narrative. Susan is the one to whom the *upward* figure is applied: as she works her way into the inner operations of the Blackett empire and rises from one responsible position to another, she is repeatedly represented as "a remarkable girl" who is "moving up the ladder." David, who is presumably an irresponsible alcoholic, is fired from one job in the Blackett complex and has a very precarious hold on another one, is described as being "on the *downward* path" and finally as having "touched bottom" when he holes up in a tramps' hideout and finds the derelict who holds the secret to the real nature of the Blackett organization. At last, the two forces that seem to be moving away from each other unexpectly come together, and the identity of Susan and David is revealed, along with their relationship to each other.

Gilbert's artful approach to such tricky handling is a reminder that the mystery is by nature a subtle business, most mystifying when indirectly presented, and that the most puzzling problem is the one we confront without being sure that there is any problem at all. A less skillful writer, or a less courageous one, would have followed the obvious approach of setting a pair of police detectives to work on the question of Blackett's wrongdoing, peeling away the mystery layer by layer in a conventional manner, but Michael Gilbert has developed a mystery around the persons and purposes of his two major characters, and in so doing has added a whole extra ingredient to the satisfaction of the suspense.

The strategies he employs in unfolding the real nature of the problem consist largely of hints and suggestions, such as Susan's repeated conferences with friends and relatives who know something about the nature of the Blackett empire, and the repeated telephone conversations between Susan and David, in which more seems to be afoot than is actually revealed. The whole question of the identity of Susan and David is, meanwhile, skillfully interwoven with the revelation of the extent of the guilt of Blackett and his associates in such fashion that neither mystery is allowed to intrude upon the other and that the resolution of both is at once surprising and satisfying.

End-Game is a police story but not a police procedural, because the customary police routines are subordinated to other and more devious methods and strategies. There is one sharp, rather depressing, insight into the police mind, in the form of a deal offered to a criminal in order to get a confession out of him, an agreement quite casually broken by the policeman when he has achieved what he wanted in the first place.

End-Game bears two stamps that have come to be Gilbert trademarks. First, there is the suspenseful escape scene (two of them, in fact), recounted in meticulous detail and prolonged to a point of almost delicious exasperation. The other is Gilbert's mastery of the vivid metaphor, most notable in one case where he represents a Mercedes as "sneering at the other cars in the car park," and another where the "bland autumn sun was apologizing for the past."

Michael Gilbert recently passed his seventieth birthday, but *End-Game* is an ample demonstration--if any is needed--that he has not passed his prime as a writer of tales of suspense. (George N. Dove)

Gary Goshgarian. *Atlantis Fire*. Avon, 1981 (first published in hardcover by Dial Press, 1980).

This book belongs to that sub-school of the Murder Mystery in Picturesque Foreign Settings most typified by *Levkas Man*, in which there are constant reminders of pre-classical humanity. Specifically here, the subject is Atlantis sunk in the sea; the evidence found (and then, of course, again lost by another earthquake along the same fault line that sunk the ancient civilization to begin with) is a small city that served as a religious center. Minoan society, known primarily through the later Greek myths, is "shown" to have been an offshoot (or surviving remnant) of Atlantis. That particular strategy of showing the modern and mundane Mystery of a murder (even when multiple) against the age-old Mysteries of Human Origins is a hard trick to bring off for the best writers without slipping into fatuousness or flatulence.

Gashgarian, as did Hammond Innes in *Levkas Man*, avoids the American sort of academic rivalry, yet manages (at times) to make the reader fear for the loss of knowledge occasioned by the wrong reasons (in this case a greed for the gold that most of the Atlantean religious objects are made from) which must be all too common in real human history. Yet (at other times) the hand of the "literary artist" manipulating puppets in that direction is all too obvious. The too obvious foreshadowing of the climactic battle between the hero and a (humanoid) bull in a cave during the early stages of the climactic earthquake is an obvious case in point.

That the author insists on following another frequent trend in modern mysteries of telling the reader "everything you wanted to know about" some unfamiliar modern occupation-- in this case scuba diving, especially undersea archaeology-- further complicates the slow-moving plot. The Hamletish self-doubts of the Graeco-American hero also act to slow the story down; the moderately acute reader will have already identified villains and have a pretty good guess as to their motivation while the hero is fretting about his divorce, the opportunities for a little extracurricular sex, or even how to merely get along with his fellow adventurers.

Recommended, *if* you are young enough not to have seen Lloyd Bridges in *Seahunt* syndicated reruns, if you like *long* books, and if your symbolism must be heavyhanded. Otherwise, not recommended. (R. Jeff Banks)

Peter Niesewand. *Fallback*. Morrow, 1982, 400 pp.

I must confess that I usually avoid the best-selling spy novel. I've found that, once a spy novel (or, for that matter, most mysteries) exceeds 300 pages, it is usually the case that the book has its plot inflated with so many gaseous passages that it is guaranteed to be bad.

Fallback concerns hard-bitten, ruthless Defense Intelligence Agency operative David Cane, who teams with brilliant computer theoretician Martin Ross to infiltrate the Soviet Union's missile defenses and reprogram them so as to defuse the threat to the United States. *Fallback* begins as a standard spy novel, but halfway through it becomes a rather blatant example of "spy-fi," a combination of science fiction and spy novel. It would be unfair to reveal the "fallback" position--

"the most secret secret of the United States, one we can't reveal for fifty years, not until we're dead and gone"--save to say that the "position" *is* science fiction, of a vein exhausted before 1938.

One wonders how much inside knowledge Niesewand really has of the spy business. His Russia seems convincing, save for the fact that his Russian hero is clearly a copy of Oleg Penkovskii. Niesewand, though, apparently has never been in Washington, a locale for much of the book. All we learn of the Defense Intelligence Agency is that it's located in Fairfax and has a gym where our heroes spend countless pages in training. Niesewand also had his characters travel "northeast" from Washington to Annapolis (the actual direction is east) to the "coast" of Chesapeake Bay (bays have *shores*, not coasts). I may be nitpicking, but if Niesewand is confused by elementary points of geography, how are we to trust his skill at showing us the inner secrets of intelligence?

Fallback is a mildly entertaining, synthetic, bloated, would-be bestseller that pales in comparison not only to the giants of the field--the Deightons and le Carrés--but also to the entertainers such as William Haggard and Gavin Lyall. A major disappointment. (C) (Martin Morse Wooster)

John Coyne. *Hobgoblin*. Putnam, 1981, 307 pp.

It had to happen. There have been Dungeons and Dragons sf novels (*Dream Park, Quag Keep*) and Dungeons and Dragons novels of maturing adolescents (*Mazes and Monsters*), but now, whether you like it or not, here is the first Dungeons and Dragons suspense novel. Worse than that, *Hobgoblin* is the first *preppie* Dungeons and Dragons suspense novel.

Scott Gardiner, attending a prep school where the curriculum consists of playing role-playing games, gets transferred to a boring high school which consists of dull greasers who love preppie-bashing. Will Scott exact his grisly revenge? Will Scott's mother, Barbara, learn the dread secrets of the mysterious Irish castle transplanted to the banks of the Hudson River? Who knows? Who cares?

Coyne has written a mechanical Had-I-But-Known Gothic, filled with cardboard characters, a ludicrous plot, and a climax that is, quite simply, one of the silliest I've ever read. *Hobgoblin* isn't suspenseful. It isn't even scary. It's just stupid. (D) (Martin Morse Wooster)

(Continued from page 32) like the first-class service as well, so I'm offering it for volume seven to subscribers in the U.S. and Canada. The cost will be $15.00, as opposed to $12.00, or an extra 50¢ per issue. If you want it, check the appropriate space on the order blank and send along the extra money.

On the subject of subscribers, I might point out that TMF now has more than four hundred paying subscribers (the non-paying subscribers being mostly publishers to whom I send the magazine free in hopes of coaxing the odd review copy out of them). When that number reaches five hundred, I will begin to pay for contributions. Not much, mind you, only a half cent per word for articles and a quarter of a cent per word for reviews, but it's a start. No pay for letters, sorry.

The Documents In the Case (Letters)

From Robin S. Walsh, 97 Colburn Dr., Poughkeepsie, NY 12603:
   In reply to David Wilkerson's letter in Volume 6, No. 3, Con Madden and Daniel Glower do not appear in Maurice Walsh's book *Danger Under the Moon*. The only series character in Walsh's works was Thomasheen James, who appeared in a series of non-mystery short stories written for *The Saturday Evening Post*.
   The main character in *Danger Under the Moon* is Dave Daunt. Anthony Boucher reviewed the book in *The New York Times* on January 13, 1957, as follows:

> Maurice Walsh's *Danger Under the Moon* is longish for a mystery novel with only one plot thread, and that of novelette dimensions: Young ticket-of-leave man, convicted of manslaughter, returns to Irish village to smoke out real killer--praying that it may not prove to be the girl he loves. But if the pace is slow and the wordage excessive, Mr. Walsh's easy Irish charm is so infectious that the patient reader will find his own reward.

   Hubin might have included at least two more of Walsh's books. *The Spanish Lady* (Lippincott, 1943) was reviewed in *The Atlantic Monthly* not as a murder mystery but "as a poetic love story in modern dress; but it cannot be denied that the action is noticeably enlivened by the appearance of the corpse."
   The opening of *The Road to Nowhere* (Stokes, 1934) finds Rogan Stuart the prime suspect in the murder of a man found strangled shortly after he and Rogan were seen brawling. Rogan is not possibly so concerned with who done it as with proving that he didn't.
   One of Walsh's other books, *The Hill Is Mine* (Stokes, 1940), is a thriller.
   During his lifetime (1879-1964), Maurice Walsh was one of Ireland's most popular and prolific authors. His short story "The Quiet Man" was made into one of the most successful films of 1952 (it starred John Wayne).
   Anyone who is interested in Walsh's work is invited to write to me. I will be glad to share the information that I have.
   [Any relation, Robin?]

From K. Arne Blom, Småskolevägen 22, S-22367 Lund, Sweden:
   TMF 6:4 is a very good issue--and one of the many good articles is the one by George N. Dove about *Gorky Park*. I have just read Mr. Dove's book *The Police Procedural* (published by Bowling Green University Popular Press, 1982) and must say that this book is one of the most important in the field. This is the first book on the police procedural mystery and a real cornerstone for anybody interested in the genre. I am full of respect for Mr. Dove.
   As I read his article in TMF it suddenly struck me: there is a Russian police procedural published in the U.S. I found it while book hunting back in 1975 in New York.
   It is *Petrovka 38*, by Julian Semyonov (first published in 1965 in the U.S., paperback 1974 by Stein and Day). This book verifies Mr. Dove's feeling that just about most police procedurals are technically alike around the world.
   Petrovka is, however, more interesting than *Gorky Park*, since it is written by a Russian writer, not an American one. It is some years since I read it, and I can remember that first I was a bit surprised that the more I read the stronger the feeling got that this was in a way 87th Precinct in Russian Drag. But suddenly one begins to see the difference and feel that those policemen are Russian ones, and they are created by a Russian writer, not by somebody who is trying to create something from outside.
   It is a very good book, well worth reading. The ending is interesting. The criminals in the book have not committed their crime against an individual being, but against the state --and therein is their greatest crime. They are traitors.
   The book gives good insight into everyday Russian policework and the way of thinking and problems in their work.

From Greg Goode, Hahnenstrasse 27, B1, Zi. 221, 5030 Hürth-Efferen, West Germany:
   I was pleased and gratified to read Walter Albert's review of William Marshall's *Sci Fi* (TMF 6:3:43, 29). Pleased because I have not read the book yet and it sounds interesting, and gratified because I had a theory about William Marshall which seems even more plausible to me now. Since his action scenes are so much like cinematic cross-cutting, and because his descriptive passages are so intensely visual and auditory, I was pretty sure that he likes and knows film. His style is very cinematic. So I'm not surprised to see that he has a plot element such as the All-Asia Science Fiction and Horror Movie Festival. I think I remember seeing that he is a TV writer, or has been.
   Here in Germany, certain crime and suspense films have opened several weeks before their debuts in the U.S. *The Soldier*, the James Glickenhaus film (which is suspiciously similar to Forsythe's *Dogs of War*) was here seven weeks at least before it got to the U.S. *I, the Jury* several weeks sooner, also.
   [*A later letter:*]
   Issues 6:4 and 6:5 came within about ten days of each other, like a one-two punch. Both very strong and useful issues. In 6:4 Walter Albert's film noir reviews gave me a wave of homesickness. All the articles were interesting and covered a wide variety of topics. And Steve Lewis's review of *Monthly*

Murders shows just how authoritative fannish writing can be. About Marvin Lachman's comments about my review of *Summer Fires*, perhaps we do not disagree totally about it. He rightly called it "totally unbelievable" and "gimmicky" (6:4:46), and I agree. In fact, in my review I mentioned the strikingly beautiful Latin woman who lived next door to the hero, as well as the sinister Oriental who enters the scene in the first ten pages, and the "science fiction-like" metal towers inside the buildings in the South Bronx (6:3:42). Perhaps I should have added that these elements were unrealistic, because they surely are.

TMF 6:5 made me want to order some back issues. Is that possible, Guy? I would certainly settle for photocopies. [*See the renewal form enclosed in this issue for availability of back issues.*]

Looking back at 6:4 makes me want to comment on Fred Isaac's article on the Kramer/Zondi saga. He did a very good job of articulating the subtleties that exist between the two men, and between them and the rest of their society. But in his introduction he said that *In the Heat of the Night* (1965) approaches prejudice through detection more closely than any previous novel. I think that Ed Lacy's *Room to Swing* (1957) and Juanita Sheridan's *Kahuna Killer* (1951) deserve mention, even if in these novels the theme of "the non-white detective (or assistant) solving what the white detectives can't or won't" is not as unified with the plots as it is in Ball's book.

From Melinda Reynolds, Rt. 2, Box 93B, Corydon, KY 42406:

I received my copy of TMF 6:5 and immediately went through it to find articles of interest to me that were printed in past issues. All that indexing must have been a monumental effort, and my compliments go to Mr. Charles K. Cook.

Although I have read and enjoyed mysteries for several years (*The Complete Sherlock Holmes* was a Christmas present when I was twelve; my parents were somewhat surprised when I asked for a book instead of a doll, but "The Red-Headed League" in my sixth-grade literature book had me hooked), I've only recently become an avid reader of Dick Francis. This was entirely due to the unrelenting urgings of a very good friend in Michigan who every so often in her letters or on the phone would mention that "you really should read Dick Francis--a combination of your two great interests: horses and mysteries." However, I resisted this excellent advice, due to the fact I simply couldn't reconcile the fact that an expert jockey could be an expert mystery writer--based on the ones I had met at Churchill Downs on my infrequent visits. In March of 1980 I found myself in something of a "reading void"; I had just finished reading everything Ellery Queen wrote (and didn't write), and Rex Stout before that, and there was nothing else that appealed to me (for some reason, I have never been able to read mysteries--or anything else, for that matter--written by women); then a box arrived from Michigan, containing books: three of them by Dick Francis, the others I forget, as they were by women writers and I ignored them. The note insisted I try a few of Francis's books, and so the first one I read was *Risk*, then *Flying Finish*, and the last one she sent, *Trial Run*. The next day I went out and bought *Whip Hand*, read it in

two hours, and was enthralled. Since then, I've tried to
locate all of Dick Francis's books in first editions (the
latent collector instinct coming to the fore). I have completed my American first editions and need only five titles
to complete the British first editions. Also, I found out
about PBS's *Mystery!* series "The Racing Game" a year too late,
but happily I managed to catch the reruns--since then I often
wondered why so little has been written on the "Racing Game"
segments; I thought they were rather well done. At any rate,
I'm always on the lookout for articles and such related to the
Francis books and "The Racing Game" series.

From Walter Albert, 7139 Meade St., Pittsburgh, PA 15208:
  Charles Shibuk very properly corrected my labeling Fritz
Lang's 1919 pair of serials *The Spiders* as *The Spies*. I don't
understand the error since I have never seen *Spione*. I am
sorry that Mr. Shibuk found *The Spiders* disappointing.
  He is also correct in pointing out that *Thieves Like Us*
cannot be a remake of *You Only Live Once*. As he says, however, the thematic similarities are fairly striking.
  I have often wondered why I am invariably addressed as
"Professor" as a prelude to a cataloguing of my sins. It
always reminds me of the particular tone of voice my father
would use at dinner when he would remind my brother to "pass
the Professor some more potatoes." I often wish I had passed
that civil service exam for the post office in 1955.

From Jim Goodrich, 61 Plains Rd., New Paltz, NY 12561:
  What a fascinating area you live in--particularly this
time of year. Cemetery *and* moor; I only have a cemetery down
the road. [*Jim's letter is dated "Halloween."*]
  What a clever pseudonym for the author of the fine piece
on Tod Hunter: David E. Funct.
  Re Marv Lachman's contribs, was amused by Peter Wolfe's
use of "Englished" in *Beams Falling*. We all know the sexual
meaning of "Frenched"; perhaps "Englished" denotes sodomy?
  One reason alleged for the paucity of old TV 'tec series
in syndication is that they are in b&w. OK for *Lucy*, but not
for *Peter Gunn*!
  I was one reader who skipped over Bleiler's analysis in
depth of Carr's *Peacock Feather Murders*--she was tickled to
death!--for the reasons stated by Marv.
  Forgot to mention my appreciation of Walter Albert's excellent "Reel Murders." Assume Donlevy was gunned down, not
Conte as stated in the *Big Combo* review, and that the typo is
your culpa, Guy. [*Nope, the culpa is Walter's if culpa there
be. I just checked the original MS, and that's the way it's
written.*] Haven't viewed the film in 25 years, so my memory
is not 99% accurate.
  Am trying to find the name of the Fritz Lang classic in
which Lee Marvin throws hot coffee in Gloria Graham's face--
à la Burr in *Raw Deal*--in my memory bank, to no avail. All
my reference books are still boxed.
  Must disagree, Walter, on Dennis O'Keefe's acting prowess.
I think he did *very* well with the roles he was trapped in.
Ella Raines had fine legs and an intriguing voice, am sure you
will agree. What sticks in my mind is Cook's drumming while

ogling her gams with his constantly amazed eyes. Oh, for the jazz life!

Since you were corrupted by the Pulpcon, Guy, I know you will publish more articles on the pulps à la Bob Sampson's always superb contributions. [*All that I can get.*]

From Linda Toole, 40 Hermitage Rd., Rochester, NY 14617:
Please, no gnashed teeth--these are only suggestions:
1. Would it be possible for Brownstone Books to bring out a reprint of TMN #9--the Rex Stout memorial issue? I despair of ever owning an original. You could probably sell quite a few copies--especially to Wolfe Pack members. Don't despair--you can always have John McAleer or myself mention it to members if no other avenue presents itself. (I for one will be mightily surprised if we ever see another copy of *The Gazette*!) [*I'm afraid it would be too much trouble to do. Just getting permissions would take scores of letters, and only one refusal would kill the whole thing.*]
2. How about a Nero Wolfe concordance? Again, I can foresee a goodly number of sales--especially if it can come out for $20-30. [*I'm working on it.*]

I share Steve Lewis's feelings about *The Talk Show Murders*. It starts out pleasantly tongue-in-cheek (like *Murder at the ABA*) then gets down to business and seems to lose its sense of humor. I think I finished it out of loyalty to Steve Allen, but I think a "B" is too high a grade.

In reply to True Rice: I am an omnivore-novice in the mystery field. My grand passions are Stout and locked-room mysteries. I enjoy Hillerman and Parker (even Kaminsky, sometimes) among others, and I long to get my hands on something by H.S. Keeler. [*You don't realize what you are saying.*] I'm not terribly fond of English mysteries (especially by female authors--please, Jane, no hate mail), except for James and Moyes. The above opinions (except for Stout and locked rooms) may be modified as I become more knowledgeable. I swear I have never knowingly read a HIBK, although I own a couple and probably will read them at some time out of a sense of duty. If I never bought another book, I probably have enough unread mysteries laying around to last me about ten years. (Please don't tell my husband. He thinks I probably have two or three hundred--and thinks that's too many.)

This is probably beating a dead horse, but I want to get my two cents in. I recently received my copy of *Twentieth Century Crime and Mystery Writers*. I'm in love, I'm intrigued, I'm awed, and I'm puzzled. How come Gregory MacDonald, Marvin Kaye, Stuart Kaminsky, C.W. Grafton (for example) aren't included? How come seemingly every book Asimov has ever written is listed, not just his mysteries? My only other criticism is the lack of a title index, although I realize this would have necessitated another volume and probably would have driven the editors and proof-readers mad. Was it omitted because it was a duplication of Hubin? [*Comments, John Reilly?*]

[*A later postcard:*]
Further readings in *Twentieth Century Crime and Mystery Writers*:
Nevil Shute, for God's sake!!!?
Okay, I found Gregory M̲cdonald--the rest holds true.
[*A later Letter:*]

TMF 6:4 was superlative: I enjoyed Dove's article about *Gorky Park*. Fred Isaac has added another author to my list with his article on McClure's South African mystery series. Earl Bargainnier had a point to make about British fidtion and made it well. Although not a pulp fan, I did enjoy Bob Sampson's article on the Duvalls.

Saving the best for last, I'm green with envy over David Funct's revelations regarding *An Orchid for a Killer*. First I have to cope with Otto Penzler's pronouncements regarding what constitutes a collection, now I have to face up to the fact that there's another Wolfe-related book I'll probably never be able to read, let alone own. My congratulations on your good fortune in owning it, and my thanks for sharing. It certainly does sound authentic and very entertaining. You can't be serious about the authorship, though. Semi-brilliant as Guy is, he's much too young to have authored a book copyright 1948!

From Ev Bleiler, writing from darkest New Jersey:

Thanks for the issue of the May-June TMF, which arrived shortly after I last wrote to you.

I found Bob Sampson's "Pirates in Candyland" fascinating, and I hope that he continues the series--or, if it is not a series, makes it one. I would be most curious to read more about the pulp *Scarlet Adventuress*, which I had never heard of.

I think that artist Frank Hamilton should study perspective a little more. Sampson describes Blue Jean Billy as "hardly 100 pounds." In the illustration she looks fit to take on Tarzan and Conan together mud wrestling.

Your comment on the Danish fan mag *Pinkerton* is enticing. If you could send me a xerox of the Wolfe article you mention, perhaps I could make something out of it. Perhaps not.

[*I sent Ev a copy and received a translation virtually by return mail. I am writing to Denmark for permission to reprint it, and if permission is forthcoming it will soon appear in these pages.*]

[*A later letter:*]

I was sorry to read Mr. Lachman's letter about my Carr article, for I now feel somewhat guilty at having damaged his pleasure. I respect his opinion very highly, of course, and his disapproval evokes some self-searching.

Yet, at the same time, I have to say that I disagree with almost everything that he says. This is now a problem, for I don't like to get caught up in arguments about what is ultimately a matter of taste and opinion, where all we can do is contradict one another. But since he asks for a direct reply, I feel I owe him one.

On his direct question, Did I think it worth while? I have to answer, yes. To me it was. I felt that I was not simply demolishing a book for the sake of demolishing, but trying to work out something: how initial carelessness and faking could snowball until it permeated a book, and what went wrong in this particular case and how it could have been avoided. I don't remember having seen such an approach before. Whether such an approach and technique are worth doing ultimately must be decided by others, for I am biased.

Now, as to this being perhaps helpful to a budding author, that was certainly not my attention. Nor would I be optimistic about this. Actually, for me, the worse sinner of the two

(Carr and editor) was the editor, for it was his job not to take at face value pompous publicity about accuracy and not to assume that the author always knows what he is talking about. If Carr, in the heat of writing, or for reasons of personal strain, or for other reasons, set up a shoddy piece of work, it was the editor's responsibility to call him on it.

Beyond this general answer, I don't know what to say without blowing up points of disagreement to the size of the Andes. But perhaps I can comment on some of my own background ideas and those I infer from Mr. Lachman's letter.

First, the value of extended negative criticism. Or its propriety. I can see two sides to this situation. On one side, an author is a public figure and when he knowingly or carelessly writes a thoroughly bad work (not just a couple of minor slips), he must expect criticism. On the other hand, authors are human, and I can certainly sympathize with the author in cases of brutality or meatgrinder tactics from the reviewer. How does one decide?

Related to this, emergent from this, what does one do about a bad work by a major writer? Should the badness be overlooked because of previous goodies--in other words review the author instead of the book--or should each book stand alone? My own feeling here is that the book is the thing wherein to trap the conscience of the sting, but I suspect that Mr. Lachman would disagree, since he mentions the general series of Carr works.

Second point. Mr. Lachman raises the question of lack of interest and usefulness to a reader. I disagree from two points of view. First, I doubt if there ever has been a magazine in which everything has been interesting to everybody, or even to a majority. I expect to skip, and I am sure others do, too. I don't think that an article should be denied publication because of the possibility that someone may skip it. Secondly, in fan writing most of us are really writing about what interests us. Of course we are pleased when others like it, but ultimately we write for ourselves and similar-minded people. We do not have to apologize or defend.

Third, Mr. Lachman sets up a dilemma of a sort: those who have not read this book should not read the article, those who have read the book will not remember it--so who is going to read the article? I don't agree at all, since this argument undercuts all reviewing or critical work. But I did have Mr. Lachman's point of view in mind somewhat: this is the reason for the length of the article. In addition to going into detail for its own sake, I wanted to give enough that the reader who has not read the book or who has forgotten it will be carried along.

Fourth, I am really surprised at Mr. Lachman's comment about rereading older books, since there is so much unread material. I try to read both old and new. Why not?

Two specific points: Who said or thought there were two shots. I do not agree. I see no indication that this was Pollard's thought. Second, the way that a cricketer bowls. Mr. Lachman may be right. I'll have to check. I did ask, but I may have misunderstood or been misinformed.

So, to the rest of the issue. I thought *Gorky Park* was a second or third rate collection of tec clichés, sloppily written, and while reading it I wondered whether it had originally been planned for Central Park and then moved to Moscow.

On David E. Funct (a pseudonym, defunct?) and Titus Lion. I think that Mr. Funct has stumbled upon a curious corner of post-World War II Australian publishing. The stands were then filled with one-shot, cheap publications which were strongly based on (sometimes a little too strongly) American and British material. I have some of these in the fields of crime, horror, and sf. They were published by such companies as Transport Publishing, Associated General Publications, Kookaburra, Currawong, and often had pictures of American movie stars on the cover. I have a couple written by a "Bella Luigi," whose prototype is easily guessed.

It is a very, very safe bet that *An Orchid for a Killer* was written in 1948 by some Australian hack as a deliberate imitation of Stout, and I would guess that Stout never knew about it. These publications were very ephemeral and seldom got out of the country. For more information, Mr. Funct might check with some of the Australian sf fans, who have tracked some of these items down.

From Dick Schubert, P.O. Box 420, Denver, CO 80201:
With respect to David Funct's excellent article "The Tod Hunter Question" (volume 6, number 4), I wonder if he realizes that Rex Stout's middle name is Todhunter (his mother's maiden name)?

From Bill Strong, 8800 Lake Nimbus Dr., Fair Oaks, CA 95628:
While only my fourth issue of *The Mystery Fancier*, volume 6, number 4, is my favorite to date. It has a good balance, even if the printing is not up to your high standards.

"The Tod Hunter Question" by David E. Funct was especially interesting, and the name Tod Hunter immediately rang a bell in the back of my mind.... There is a very substantial connection between Rex Stout and Tod Hunter! In John McAleer's *Rex Stout: A Biography* (Little, Brown, 1977), the relationship becomes very clear very quickly. Rex Stout's mother's maiden name is Lucetta Todhunter.

According to McAleer, the first Todhunter came to America in 1687. John Todhunter came from Cumberland, the border region between Scotland and England. The region also "gave rise to the calling that gave them their name, tod hunters, hunters of foxes--not a sport, but an earnest undertaking. Foxes killed many sheep each year and men were paid good bounties to kill them" (p. 25).

The McAleer book offers other startling items of interest concerning the biographical note in the Auguts 22, 1930 *Detective Fiction Weekly*, such as the following: Rex Stout was born in Noblesville, Indiana, in 1886, but the family moved to Topeka, Kansas, a year later. Thus the Topeka, Kansas, reference.

As for being a direct descendant of a petty officer on the *Mayflower*, that is typical Stout wit at work. Chapter 11 of McAleer's book is entitled "The Mayflower Years." I will provide some of the relevant details of that chapter below:

On July 12, 1905, Rex Stout ran away or just left home and joined the Navy. He signed up in Pittsburgh, Kansas, and took his training in Brooklyn and Norfolk on the *Hancock* and the *Franklin*. At yeomans school he was trained as a bookkeeper.

As luck would have it, he was then assigned to the *Mayflower*, President Theodore Roosevelt's official yacht as the payyeoman. McAleer's description of his two years abord the *Mayflower* are delightful and alone are well worth the price of the book. "On 8 July 1907, while the *Mayflower* was visiting New York, Rex asked permission to buy his discharge, an option open to men who had served at least two years of their four year enlistment." Thus ended Rex Stout's naval career and may very well have given birth to "a direct descendent of a petty officer on the *Mayflower*."

In reference to the claim of football coach, Stout was always fabricating stories about his prowess as a football player and by 1930 that may have grudually progressed from player to coach as middle age approached.

Other jobs Stout tried after the Navy included window dresser, tobacco-store salesman, bellhop, motorman, tugboat worker, bookkeeper (several times), barker on a Manhattan sightseeing bus, plumber's assistant in Pittsburgh, cook in Duluth, book salesman in Chicago, seller of baskets and blankets on a Navaho reservation outside Santa Fe, and hotel manager in St. Louis. It is also believable for Stout to call himself an actor, since McAleer states on page 160 that "one year the Stout family players put on a complete vaudeville show."

The comment about authoring several other books outside the mystery field, including "a psychiatric jokebook called *Mind Chasm*" could be a reference by Stout to his first novel, *How Like a God*, which was published in 1929. According to McAleer, in *How Like a God* "the story is told while the protagonist is mounting the stairs to kill his mistress. As he climbs he reviews the circumstances that have led him to this moment." The book got mixed reviews, many of which referred to the novel in such terms as exploring "the dark regions of sex psychoses" and "a brilliant conception of modern human psychoses" (p. 212). Sounds like "Mind Chasms" would be a typical Stout witicism for *Detective Fiction Weekly* in 1930.

Interestingly enough, McAleer's checklist at the back of his book does not list any fictional work for Stout published in magazines after "Heels of Fate" *All-Story Weekly*, November 17, 1917. It is hard to believe that Stout did not continue to produce some mystery short stories at least up to 1934 when his first mystery, *Fer-de-Lance*, was published. Very possibly Tod Hunter provided the anonymous device to generate both experience and pin money. Or should I say pen money?

From John L. Apostolou, 425 S. Kenmore Ave. #310, Los Angeles, CA 90020.

The first time through David E. Funct's "The Tod Hunter Question" in TMF 6·4, I thought that the author had set forth an interesting thesis. I was puzzled, however, by Funct's failure to mention that W.T. Ballard and Rex Stout were related--cousins I believe. But then I noticed that the picture of Tod Hunter on page three looked familiar. It is actually a photo of pulp writer Robert Reeves, creator of Cellini Smith, from the dust jacket of *Dead and Done For* (Knopf, 1939). And when I learned that "Wolf Trap" by Tod Hunter was not listed in E.R. Hagemann's index to *Black Mask*, I realized that I was the victim of a clever and amusing hoax.

DAPA-EM and David E. Funct may have pulled "a fast one," but they are certainly far from defunct.

From Dave Lewis, 8750 North Columbia Boulevard, #8, Portland, OR 97203, letter of 7 June 1982:
Dear Guy,
Here at last is "The Tod Hunter Question." Hope you are able to decipher my pasted together revision. The only thing in this package I would like back is the original paste-up for *An Orchid for a Killer*. Eventually I may have to show it to some would-be traders. I have already had one serious offer for the book from a guy not in the apa.
I was amazed at the number of people who seem to have believed it. [...]
So, to make as few new enemies as possible, it may be a good idea to use a pen name for *The Mystery Fancier*. What do you think of "The Tod Hunter Question" by David E. Funct? If no one else identifies me in the following couple of issues, you or I could do it.
To explain it you might use a line like this at the end: (This article originally appeared in the fanzine *Fast One* in March, 1982, in the 45th mailing of DAPA-EM.)
I think it's only fair to give your readers the "fast one" hint.

(Continued from page 22)

DEATH OF A MYSTERY WRITER

Frederic Dannay at age 76 in White Plains, New York, 4 September 1982. He was famous as one half of the Ellery Queen team and had, for over forty years, edited *Ellery Queen's Mystery Magazine*.

James A. Brussel at age 77 in New York City, 21 October 1982. He was a psychiatrist who had testified at many famous criminal trials, including those of George Metesky ("the mad bomber") and Albert H. De Salvo ("the Boston strangler"). He wrote of his experiences in *Confessions of a Crime Psychiatrist* (1968). He also wrote one mystery novel, *Just Murder, Darling* (1959), an interesting effort told from the criminal's viewpoint. Brussel was also a former assistant commissioner of the New York State Department of Mental Hygiene.

Richard Jessup at age 57 in Nokomis, Florida, 22 October 1982. He had been a merchant seaman, but in 1948 he gave that up to become a full-time writer. Between 1954 and 1963 he published about ten paperback original mysteries for Dell and Gold Medal. Then, in 1964, he achieved success for his gambling novel, *The Cincinnati Kid*, which was turned into a very popular film with Steve McQueen, Edward G. Robinson, and Ann Margaret.

U.S. Postal Service
STATEMENT OF OWNERSHIP, MANAGEMENT AND CIRCULATION
Required by 39 U.S.C. 3685)

1A. TITLE OF PUBLICATION	1B. PUBLICATION NO.	2. DATE OF FILING
The Mystery Fancier	4 2 8 5 9 0	11 November 1982

3. FREQUENCY OF ISSUE	3A. NO. OF ISSUES PUBLISHED ANNUALLY	3B. ANNUAL SUBSCRIPTION PRICE
Bi-monthly	6	$12.00

4. COMPLETE MAILING ADDRESS OF KNOWN OFFICE OF PUBLICATION *(Street, City, County, State and ZIP Code) (Not printers)*

Guy M. Townsend, 1711 Clifty Drive, Madison, IN 47250 (Jefferson County)

5. COMPLETE MAILING ADDRESS OF THE HEADQUARTERS OF GENERAL BUSINESS OFFICES OF THE PUBLISHER *(Not printer)*

Same

6. FULL NAMES AND COMPLETE MAILING ADDRESS OF PUBLISHER, EDITOR, AND MANAGING EDITOR *(This item MUST NOT be blank)*

PUBLISHER *(Name and Complete Mailing Address)*

Same

EDITOR *(Name and Complete Mailing Address)*

Same

MANAGING EDITOR *(Name and Complete Mailing Address)*

Same

7. OWNER *(If owned by a corporation, its name and address must be stated and also immediately thereunder the names and addresses of stockholders owning or holding 1 percent or more of total amount of stock. If not owned by a corporation, the names and addresses of the individual owners must be given. If owned by a partnership or other unincorporated firm, its name and address, as well as that of each individual must be given. If the publication is published by a nonprofit organization, its name and address must be stated.) (Item must be completed.)*

FULL NAME	COMPLETE MAILING ADDRESS
Guy M. Townsend (sole owner)	1711 Clifty Drive, Madison, IN 47250

8. KNOWN BONDHOLDERS, MORTGAGEES, AND OTHER SECURITY HOLDERS OWNING OR HOLDING 1 PERCENT OR MORE OF TOTAL AMOUNT OF BONDS, MORTGAGES OR OTHER SECURITIES *(If there are none, so state)*

FULL NAME	COMPLETE MAILING ADDRESS
None	

9. FOR COMPLETION BY NONPROFIT ORGANIZATIONS AUTHORIZED TO MAIL AT SPECIAL RATES *(Section 423.12 DMM only)*
The purpose, function, and nonprofit status of this organization and the exempt status for Federal income tax purposes *(Check one)*

(1) ☐ HAS NOT CHANGED DURING PRECEDING 12 MONTHS (2) ☐ HAS CHANGED DURING PRECEDING 12 MONTHS *(If changed, publisher must submit explanation of change with this statement.)*

10. EXTENT AND NATURE OF CIRCULATION	AVERAGE NO. COPIES EACH ISSUE DURING PRECEDING 12 MONTHS	ACTUAL NO. COPIES OF SINGLE ISSUE PUBLISHED NEAREST TO FILING DATE
A. TOTAL NO. COPIES *(Net Press Run)*	667	700
B. PAID CIRCULATION 1. Sales through dealers and carriers, street vendors and counter sales	65	75
2. Mail Subscription	380	427
C. TOTAL PAID CIRCULATION *(Sum of 10B1 and 10B2)*	445	502
D. FREE DISTRIBUTION BY MAIL, CARRIER OR OTHER MEANS SAMPLES, COMPLIMENTARY, AND OTHER FREE COPIES	90	15
E. TOTAL DISTRIBUTION *(Sum of C and D)*	535	517
F. COPIES NOT DISTRIBUTED 1. Office use, left over, unaccounted, spoiled after printing	132	183
2. Return from News Agents	0	0
G. TOTAL *(Sum of E, F1 and 2—should equal net press run shown in A)*	667	700

11. I certify that the statements made by me above are correct and complete

SIGNATURE AND TITLE OF EDITOR, PUBLISHER, BUSINESS MANAGER, OR OWNER

Guy M. Townsend, Editor

PS Form 3526 July 1982 *(See instruction on reverse)*

www.ingramcontent.com/pod-product-compliance
Lightning Source LLC
Chambersburg PA
CBHW031432040426
42444CB00006B/780